CHAMELEON SKILLS

THOMAS FAUSTMAN

amalgam

Published by Amalgam Studio LLC, Chicago

Names have been changed to protect the guilty.

Amalgam Studio publishes its books in physical and electronic formats. Some content that appears in print may not be available in electronic books, and vice versa. For more information about Amalgam Studio products, please visit our website www.amalgamstudio.com.

ISBN-13 978-0-9845688-0-2

Printed in the United States of America

1 2 3 4 5 6 7 8 9 10

To my Dad who gave me the writing genes and my angel face, who outwits me daily. But does it tastefully.

TABLE OF CONTENTS

SECTION 1: EARLY STAGES OF WORK LIFE

SECTION 2: MIDDLE MANAGEMENT - ADVANCED SKILLS

SECTION 3: EXECUTIVE LEVEL

SECTION 4: CONCLUSION

INTRODUCTION

Per Webster's, a chameleon "is a lizard that has the ability to vary the color of its skin." While hardly a flattering self-portrait, this is God's creature that best visualizes how I maneuvered the chaotic maze called "The Business World."

I graduated as an English major from a small Liberal Arts college. Then I was drafted by the Army and astoundingly placed in the Military Police. When I asked why the Army thought I was MP material, I was told "because you don't have a criminal record." As I was puzzling over that, the rascals sent me to Vietnam. I mention this chronology to show my meager background when starting my first job in a large insurance company.

As a B.A. in Literature, my exposure to business training in college was nil. My thought was a businessman was someone unlucky enough not to get a teaching or coaching job. Didn't these business characters have to work all summer? The only guidance I got at home was "learn to read and write and you'll be way ahead of most people." This simple advice seemed pointless then but proved prophetic.

I'm not being self-effacing when describing my state of preparation for working in any business let alone a major insurance company. This book describes over (30) years of practical learning that led me to a senior vice-presidential level in a Fortune 100 corporation where I managed over 6,000 people that included lawyers, doctors, MBA's and actuaries.

I never got advanced degrees, read management books judiciously and had little outside professional training. What I did do is outlined in the following pages. The book addresses the common stages of a career and the required skills, wily techniques, covert practices and occasional sacrifices needed to excel. You may note a certain irreverent tone to my writing. That's because there is certain irreverence to my life. I call it charm; others call it a genetic defect.

Although the book is written from a male point of view,

the principles are gender neutral. My wife and daughters practice these approaches and are outmaneuvering their competitors as you read this book. Business school and business degrees are very useful but common sense can take you a long way.

SECTION 1

EARLY STAGE OF WORK LIFE

1. ENTERING A CAREER

"Yea though I walk through the valley of death, I will fear… "

I WAS TERRIFIED when starting work that first day at a large insurance company. As a former MP in Vietnam, my new employer thought me a natural for investigating disability insurance claims. The theory was "if he could fight the Viet Cong, then he should be able to sniff-out a malingerer." My first project was learning what "malingerer" meant.

Most of us are relieved just to get a job. The early days of our career are full of learning the basics of "the job" and being content that the paycheck rolls in bi-weekly. If the office cafeteria is great, you can be rather happy for months or years. Money in your pocket, good chow, nice desk and no one shoots at you- at least not literally. What's not to like?

Then the "A" word grows like a master malingerer's

waistline. By the way, "A" means AMBITION. Some of us notice that others have nicer chairs, get a peek out a window, don't have air vents blowing their hair into left field and rarely have to schlep coffee for the boss. If you notice these disgruntled symptoms, and get irritated, the bug of ambition has bitten you. Everything changes after this initial wound. But what do you do about it?

Mentoring didn't get invented yet so I watched and studied those supervisors above me that had the nicest perks. What did they have that made them successful? What were common traits? What was their style? How did they dress? Could I do what they did? Was I willing to make changes? Wasn't I superior to these pathetic mopes? How would I make people notice me?

2. HONEST SKILL ASSESSMENT

"I know I'm perfect, but if tortured, what would I reluctantly agree is weak?"

TAKING A HARD LOOK AT YOUR WEAKNESSES is painful. We tend to minimize our poor skills and exaggerate strengths. I'm pettier than most, so I stand as testament that it can be done. My technique went as follows:

1. Put your strengths and weaknesses on a piece of paper.
2. Find a friend you trust to review and endorse your analysis.
3. Get rid of that friend.
4. Determine what realistically can be changed/improved.
5. Think how strengths can be maximized.
6. Avoid situations where your weaknesses will be visible.

I had some glaring negatives when I completed my self-flagellation. No formal business training in college. No money to buy good clothes. No great role models at work. Wasn't a gifted dancer. No public speaking skill or confidence. I could go on but you got the point. Was I a hopeless loser or could I climb from the dumpster?

Rather than wallow in self-defeat, I focused on what I could control. More than anything, I had a strong desire to get promoted and make more money. I wasn't satisfied being "one of the drones" and wanted the self-satisfaction of becoming successful. I was naturally competitive and enjoyed a good struggle. I was ready to begin the fight. In hindsight, I made many good moves and these actions start the first lesson.

(Note that I wasn't this bright or mature at age 26 and my actions were mostly instinct, common sense and desperation and only became clear to me as effective years afterwards.)

3. CONSCIOUS DECISION TO SUCCEED

"Why doesn't everyone recognize how sharp I am and just pay me what I'm really worth?"

WHEN I WAS IN GRADE SCHOOL, there was a weird kid that actually paid me to play with him after school. This was a grand arrangement but it wasn't secure employment or enough cash to get me by in the adult world. I needed more control. I couldn't wait for someone to notice me. People don't spend much time wondering what they can do to help someone else's career. The most important step was saying out loud:

1. "I'm not satisfied with what I have."
2. "I want more."

3. "I want to get ahead."
4. "I will get a promotion."
5. "I'm going to change!"
6. "Why can't I dance like John Travolta?"

(Be careful not to yell these phrases in the office or you will hurt the cause.)

Once committed to advancement, this desire should steer your every action. This ambition can't be one-day frenzy. Everything you do thereafter should be linked to achieving the prize. There must be a passion burning each day that smolders steadily. Many of your peers will erupt brightly for short periods then fizzle into dormancy. Now that you have the passion, what do you do next?

4. DRESS

"If you look good, chances are you are good."

PEOPLE JUDGE YOU by your appearance. Weird-looking people (most don't recognize their inclusion in this bunch) start behind the eight ball. The easiest change you can make to maximize your impact is in your clothes. Sometimes your immediate boss might not dress much better than you. (This will become an advantage later on! I had a manager who frequently wore a seersucker suit in the summer. Sadly, this boss always sat with his legs spread widely and displaying a huge, murky urine stain.) It's best to look at how the top person in your office dresses and mimic them. You can tell general styles whether the leader is male or female. Do they dress conservatively or trendy? A Zorro cape or leopard hat is a dead giveaway to your boss's leanings.

Here are some basic rules:

1. If in doubt, go conservative.
2. Dress better than your peers
3. Shine your shoes
4. Wear darker colors
5. Make sure your leathers (shoes, belts) match color
6. Make sure your clothes are pressed.
7. Buy what you can afford, but make sure it's well tailored.
8. Don't go native on casual day
9. If someone tries to buy a bagel from you, you failed.

Vignette

When I managed a large mid-western office for an insurance company, my assistant manager asked me if I ever noticed that Roger (a minion) wore the same clothes as me. Roger was a victim of one of my dress for success lectures and decided imitation was easier than imagination. On review, I had to admit that my clone had the exact shoes, blue suit, white shirt, camel overcoat and red tie. Roger was ½ a foot smaller than me and looked like a shrunken Mini-Me.

The lesson is that Roger went too far. He listened to what I said but was too literal. Everyone in the office laughed at him and he undid the positives he strove for. You can dress similarly to other successful managers and no one will notice. If you become a clone, you risk looking like an idiot. Sadly, Roger didn't last long in the corporate world. I think he bought a condo in Iraq.

5. STUDY YOUR BOSS

I HAD EVERY STEREOTYPICAL BOSS IMAGINABLE. The range went from Napoleonic gnome to self-proclaimed genius. When you learned their style, you took the first step toward control. The key is to know what your boss likes. Here are the classic middle manager types and suggestions for gaining advantage:

Jock

Find out what sport they like and learn as much as you can about their beloved hobby. Talk about it as much as possible. Try to get tickets to an event and go with them. Ask lots of questions so they can display their expertise. If you play against them, avoid beating them and, if you do, feign shock at the outcome.

Chatty

This type likes to hear their voice. They tend to be an expert on everything. Let these people go on and remain an active listener. Make certain you show visible interest in what they are saying. Interject frequently but let them lead the conversation.

Organized

Neat piles and spiffy reports rule here. Make certain your desk is always neat. Joke about poor souls who claim they can find everything on their chaotic, windswept workstation. Find the format the boss wants and never be late.

Aggressive

This boss can be dangerous. Could have personal problems or might be just mean. Regardless, you should always look them straight in the eye and answer crisply. If they complain about something or someone, don't argue. Stay neutral but don't disagree with the boss. Let them see you are aggressive too-but never top them. They like being the toughest.

Indecisive

Many bosses got to the middle level by just being there

longest. These wafflers hate complex situations and dread multiple paths. Jump in, offer opinions and take responsibility. They will give you all you can handle.

Pal

This boss likes being liked. Under threat of death, the loveable leader won't correct or criticize their people. As they are being led to the guillotine, the chummy boss will tell the axeman not to feel bad. Play this boss like you're best buddies. You will quickly climb over them but no bridge was burned. Don't worry about hurting their feelings- this happy boss will be thrilled for you.

Vignette

Harvey was a nervous peer of mine. We worked for Norm, who was a nasty combination of military brat, anal-retentive, over-organization and aggression. Norm liked everything on time and buttoned-down. Surprise was only for losers.

On a field trip, Harvey volunteered to drive Norm to the airport when a meeting ran long and the departure time was at risk. Speeding down the interstate, Norm complained from the back seat that "it was too hot and hit the AC." Harvey fumbled with the strange rental car and hit the hood release by accident. After minutes of knuckle-grinding rear view mirror maneuvering, we eased to the breakdown lane. Norm invented new levels of profanity as he berated Harvey and banished him to the back seat as I finished the drive. I got us to the airport safely and knew Harvey's NASCAR dream was over.

There are subsets but most bosses fit these categories. Never let them know you are aware of their predictability. We all think we're unique. No boss likes to have his or her bubble burst. Keep your eyes open and make them feel special.

6. MAKING THE BOSS LOOK GOOD

"There is never a lack of effort when there is glory to be grabbed."

It took me awhile to realize that my boss controlled pay raises, incentive payments, stock option awards, seating placement, vacation approval, aggravation dispersion etc. These are all wonderful things that you can influence if you play smart. Most of my peers whined about everything. They dumped all their woes on the boss. Who likes being a toxic whine dump?

People also like to take credit for everything. If there is praise being bestowed, most workers seem magnetized for self-adulation. Conversely, if something goes wrong, people vanish like the Cubs at playoff time.

There is another fallacy that the boss "really wants to know what is going on." The reality is the boss only wants to know what's going on "if it will make me look either good or bad." Get any bad news to them quickly with suggestions for damage control. If the plan works, give them the credit.

If the news is good, help the boss act humble and self-effacing. Offer to hold the mirror as they practice looking surprised. While I'm being a bit tongue in cheek here, most leaders love accepting the glory.

Tips:

1. Praise your boss publicly; it will get back to him/her
2. Praise your boss to their boss.
3. If the boss screws something up, try to take blame for them.
4. Make sure the boss knows you took the bullet.
5. Avoid being a flagrant ass-kisser.

Vignette

John was notoriously inept with cars or anything mechanical. He did everything possible to avoid driving anyone anywhere or running audiovisual equipment. One freezing winter day, John got stuck driving his largest client back to the airport. John was a good boss so I volunteered to do the chauffeuring if I could use his car. John got his wheels from the office garage and left it out-front of the building.

Unfortunately, he left the car running and locked the keys inside. The customer arrived shortly and I took the blame for the bumbling. They were gracious and waited patiently as the lot attendant with burglary skills popped the lock. I told John of the mishap and made certain it was a lighthearted rendition so he didn't feel stupid. That was a generous bonus year!

7. KNOWING THE BOSS' SCHEDULE

After determining the leader's style, you need to study their schedule. Are they in early or late? Do they leave early or late? You need to mimic the same schedule so the boss thinks you are as sensible as they are. The most important practice is staying "almost" as late as the boss and being seen. Let them outlast you most nights. Make certain you say goodnight and shake your head in admiration at their diligence.

Some leaders don't trust people that are in early. Too blue collar. Maybe an unconscious desire to be a milkman? Work from home if you need the extra hours but don't make the late arriving leader look bad because you come in early. We all like people who are like us. Not better than us but a humble version of the masterpiece.

Vignette

I transferred to the Midwest for my first major management assignment. My boss told me to seek advice from the senior manager in the same city. "Len is the finest manager I've ever met. He is a legend in our business." I called Len faithfully each morning to set up a meeting and always got a call back when I wasn't around. This went on for weeks.

I finally set a lunch meeting so I could drink from the font of wisdom. Len suggested, "A buffet place in a downtown hotel." We met and I was underwhelmed by the legend. He ate voraciously and gave almost no business insight. I offered to pay the bill but Len shook his head and said, "They think we're staying at the hotel so we don't have to pay."

I was intrigued and began studying Len. I found he arrived to work most mornings around 10:30 am and checked for messages. He then took the newspaper and went to the men's room to do his constitutional and to ponder the mysteries on the sports page. Next came a two-hour lunch at the innumerable hotels where he did the guest trick like Houdini. Before leaving around 4pm, he always called his boss on the East Coast to chat. They traded war stories before bidding adieu. (Len was trying to prevent his boss from calling later that day, only to find him gone early.)

If anyone called Len early or late, his secretary was instructed to say, "He's travelling to his other office, has a doctor's appointment or is doing some charitable work." His assistant was a master at never using the same excuse twice in a row. Len was to be reached at home if anyone was too important or persistent.

I mention this episode not as exemplary but to underline what was the finest mastery of knowing your boss's schedule. Len retired a few years later and can be viewed slipping furtively into some buffet line as we speak.

8. LIKEABILITY

THIS IS A GROSSLY UNDERESTIMATED SKILL. Some are born likeable but most of us need to work at it. Most leaders surround themselves with different styles and skills but rarely do they have people in the inner circle they dislike. We spend most of our waking hours at work and being with A-holes is religiously avoided.

Your honest assessment skills are needed again. Are people at ease in your presence? Do they smile and make eye contact with you? Do they tend to stop and chat with you? Do you get invited to important meetings? Do people ask you for advice? If you struggle to say yes to any of these questions, you need some help.

Traits of likeable people:

1. Humor
2. Good listener
3. Engaged but not intense
4. Honest and constructive
5. Not judgmental
6. Manly or womanly -but not macho or a diva
7. Thoughtful
8. Positive
9. Have all the above traits but are not widely hated.

If in doubt, the boss will promote someone they like even if the competitor is slightly more qualified. Count on that. A few more notes about humor.

Relax; you don't have to be a comedian. I'm talking about people that make you laugh or laugh with you. Work isn't full of yuks so it's a treat to belly laugh about something and break the tension or tedium. Many people equate wit with intelligence. Think what a compliment it is to be called "clever." However, carried to an extreme, humor can be viewed as silly or frivolous. You don't want a reputation for not taking anything seriously.

Vignette

I worked with Bob early in my career. Bob was hysterically funny and we became great friends. I noticed that everyone stopped at his office and stayed forever yuking it up. I wished I could be funny like Bob. One day Bob stopped at my office and told me the boss called him in for a little counseling.

"Bob, you're the kind of guy that if I pointed out the window at your apartment and said it was on fire, you'd laugh." Bob started to chuckle. The boss shook his head sadly. "See Bob, you're a little rough around the edges. You need to tighten up!" Tongue-in-cheek, Bob asked me, "Do you think that lecture was a positive or a negative?" Bob went on to great success but he toned himself down from that day forward.

Here are my thoughts on practical joking. I started my career as a relentless practical joker. People like practical jokes as long as they are not victims. It's fun to work with someone who does funny stunts and relieves the tedium. However, there are a few rules and the higher you go in a career the less you can be a practical joker. People want their leaders to be serious and reliable. Jokers are unpredictable.

Practical Joke Rules:

- Never play jokes on a superior.
- Never do anything physically harmful
- Never play sexual pranks with the opposite sex.
- Stop the jokes when you reach management level

Vignette

Ron was one of my first managers. He was an Ivy League grad and spoke, dressed and wrote well. Ron was also a major ball-buster. Nobody was safe from his razor sharp wit. I was the aim of one his best pranks. Ron got all my personal information and filed a fictitious health claim for my "venereal warts." I got questions sent home and my wife got the mail before me. Do I need to say more? I needed revenge.

I noticed that Ron went to the bathroom a lot. Nothing serious, he just did #2 frequently. Almost like clockwork, I observed. The manager of the office (Ron's boss) was older and peed almost constantly. (Nice work environment, huh?) The bathrooms were centered in the building and had no windows. Got pitch dark when you turned the lights out.

I kept watching and lightning struck. Ron went to the head and I followed. As Ron entered the stall and dropped his drawers, I turned off the lights and left Ron in the dark.

As I walked away, the older boss was walking down the hallway and entered the blackened bathroom, flipped on the lights, and found Ron halfway to the lights-- with his pants down. Tough situation to explain to your boss. "Now tell me again, why are you standing in the dark with your pants off?"

Unfortunately, I got spotted walking away at the momentous moment and got called into the boss. The elder leader admitted it was funny but told me "your sense of humor will get you in trouble one day." This was sage advice and both Ron and I settled into a boring, but professional, routine.

9. POSITIVE APPROACH

How irritating it is to always hear reasons why something can't be done. While you should avoid a yes-man reputation, you should err on being too "can-do." Strong leaders tend to surround themselves with workers that get things done. It takes guts to do the difficult. Who needs people that always say no?

When confronted with a demand that seems impossible, delay before you say it can't be done. One technique is to say you are happy to do the work. Then say you want to discuss the factors that make the task prone to failure. Tell the boss that you will do it anyway but the result might not be what was expected.

Ask the boss if they see any other risks that might affect the outcome. Many times the boss will nix the job when hearing the negatives out loud. You get some residual credit for keeping the boss out of trouble but you were still positive.

Vignette

Terry was very bright, assertive and articulate (good things) but she always had a million questions about a task and became vehement in arguing every point before agreeing to the assignment.

One day the boss sat beside her and said, "Terry, you have a very annoying trait that I'd like to discuss. You always answer my question with a question." Terry said peevishly, "What do you mean? Can you give me one concrete example?" Terry was gone at the end of the week. I think she works in Abu Garib prison as an interrogator.

Technique - "There is always a solution"

Being positive will only get you so far. You have to get results or attitude is just for show. I learned to approach problems with the "there is always a solution" technique. (No, I wasn't smoking anything.) My method was to visualize the ideal outcome then work backward to define the individual steps. Once you determine there is a feasible answer, refining the detail follows much easier.

What do you do when the final resolution escapes you? If there isn't a perfect solution, then find what the next best outcome is. Tell your manager what you considered, what you think is a realistic result, and get their buy-in. If your boss can't come up with an answer, then they can't fault you.

Vignette

One of the companies I worked for signed a long-term lease right before a real estate recession. Our monthly rent charges were ludicrous. I was asked to play Solomon and solve the financial conundrum. After reading the lease, I knew we were hosed legally. Then I met the leasing company's landlord and knew we were hosed literally. This guy actually enjoyed telling me how to pound sand. Screwed, right?

My recommendation was to achieve a new level of "high maintenance." We began to bombard the landlord with service requests. Thing likes "the elevators squeak", "freakish Sahara-hot winds inside the office space", "peregrine falcon attacks in the garage", "noxious and loathsome smells in the restrooms", "unsavory interlopers in the stairwells" began to pepper the landlord's in-box. We were creative and relentless. It took about a year but they were glad to see us leave. There is always a way.

10. FAILURE

"It's okay to fail--as long as you weren't the one that failed."

ALL THE BUSINESS SCHOOLS and management books tell you to be a risk taker. "Get out there and get things done." "It's okay to make mistakes." "The creative process includes more failure than victory." "People like workers who try new ideas, even it they fail sometimes." "We'd never reach the stars if it weren't for failure."

This is pure bullshit.

Our whole society shuns losers. Do we have parades for the Superbowl loser? What are tolerated are infrequent mistakes that are rapidly admitted and fixed. Then you need to have long periods of success before the screw-up is forgotten. Flagrant failure is never forgiven or forgotten. Don't be lured into this trap. Avoid situations that offer high failure rates.

Vignette

Wally was an account executive travelling to Atlanta for a major sales presentation to a Fortune 500 prospect. Wally was very cocky and viewed himself a world traveler. When he landed in Atlanta, he got the rental car and declined directions or maps.

We waited and waited for Wally to show for the practice session. Then we waited for Wally to arrive for the live presentation. No Wally to be found. We were all worried but were relieved the next day in the office when we saw Wally sitting at his desk.

"Where were you?" "Why didn't you show for the meeting?" Wally chuckled and admitted that he made a wrong turn and ended up in South Carolina. He kept driving because he didn't want "to look stupid asking for directions." Then he realized that he'd never make the presentation on time "so he went home."

Wally did the noble thing and admitted a mistake. He was brutally honest about his actions and actually seemed amused by the episode. Wally was also unemployed after that discussion. This was one of those times when the truth would kill you. Why not a more creative story about an

18-wheeler pile-up or biblical pestilence? Wally remains a legend of honest miscalculation.

Mistakes happen

While failure should be avoided at all cost, there are always some mistakes. Most of these miscues are not disastrous and can be overcome. When you are clearly at fault and the outcome will be visible, admit the error immediately and apologize. Most people get defensive and never accept blame for mistakes. It is refreshing to encounter someone who accepts ownership. If you do this mea culpa sincerely and take steps to minimize the negative outcome, you often get sympathy and a reputation for honesty. Everyone feels bad for you.

Vignette

After my career as a malingerer investigator blossomed, I was promoted to supervisor. My job was to oversee the disability unit, review the reports and issue checks to the walking wounded. One of the typists asked me to review a file that noted "the phone booth on 8th and Chestnut" as the mailing address. I knew it was odd but OK'd the check. I admit the oddness of it amused me.

Months later an auditor found this less than kosher. I could have blamed it on "clerical error" since we had huge typists' turnover. Rather than be defensive, I looked at the auditor and said, "Yes, I approved it. I thought he was Superman and didn't want to piss him off."

After the auditor laughed, I also gave him more detail on other unique mail situations we dealt with routinely. This retort became part of my legend and they overlooked my poor judgement. I was a bit lucky that a funny answer was so obvious and the auditor had a sense of humor. Luck is a good thing.

11. HUMAN RESOURCES

When I started work, I first encountered "The Personnel Department." Coming from the Army, this seemed an appropriately unimpressive, dismissive term for "people." It would have been mundane to call it the People Department, so the Personnel Department was invented.

I noticed a trend that whenever the economy got lousy, canny business folks often changed the name of their people. Suddenly we became "Human Resources." The bad news was that downsizing (called "rightsizing" when you actually meet with the people being canned) was driving the fancy title change. It was tough to get rid of people but a resource (like anthracite coal or dried guano) was a snap.

Later we became "Human Capital" and a new round of heads rolled. This was a clever way to tell managers that people are precious, like gold bars, and who in their right mind wants too much bullion lying around? When you met with the "capital", you told them "their function was eliminated." Nothing personal, it's just that your finicky function just went and got obsolete. I hate when functions cause problems.

WORTHLESS HR FUNCTIONS

Deliver the "Corporate Message"

Each year the message must change. Senior leaders worry about being accused of "not thinking outside the box" or lacking "strategic vision" if they don't switch signals yearly. HR people are responsible that everyone in the corporation hears and memorizes the new direction. Trick quizzes and public humiliation for those failing to recite accurately is the preferred method.

"HR Speak"

It takes special people to create acronyms, buzzwords and business jargon. The best HR people can string full paragraphs together without using one word that lay people would understand. Things like, "The Hercules PDP queue was marginalized when the process champion acted as a liaison to the business owner but never got VOC validation" roll off their tongue.

Create Forms

This can be lifetime employment if you make forms complicated enough. The key is making forms vital but impossible to complete without expert help. A great form can delineate the various levels of non-performers and prevent anyone from being promoted. I've seen a form with (9) different blocks for crappy work. My favorite was "ill-suited for job but has high potential."

VALUABLE HR FUNCTIONS

Management advice

Everyone likes to discuss new ideas or business philosophy with a trusted associate. It is rare that you can have these conversations with a peer or superior. Hence, the sage HR manager can fill the void. When you find this savvy ear, befriend them for life. You want someone who challenges you, has independent thoughts and knows business realities.

Influencing promotion

The HR guru I described above is also likely to have the senior leaders trust. Good companies maintain succession-planning lists. Ask your HR confidant about the lists and determine where you are placed. If not a player, solicit suggestions for more favorable positioning. Who do you need to impress? What is that leader looking for that you lack? Find a way to get in front of that influential person with your new, improved image. This is a big deal. Get working!

Vignette

Early in my sales career, I was a lower level salesman working (a few layers down) for Mel, who was a legend in our business. Mel could sell a thong to Donny Rumsfeld but he was a difficult guy "to read" or predict. Each sales team had to present client plans to Mel before each meeting and get his sign-off before proceeding. None of us had much luck getting his blessing.

I consulted the HR manager since he worked with Mel for years and had a great relationship. "Mel gets bored easily. If you see him tugging on his collar he's getting irritated. If he tugs on the collar and starts jerking his head back and forth that means 'you're really starting to piss me off' and you better change gears. If he tugs, jerks then looks out the window, you better get the hell out of there. He likes things short and sweet."

The next presentation with Mel was successful. I was crisp, vigilant of the tug, jerk and window glance, and moved to new points if the body language began. My peers remained baffled and continued as victims of Mel's low boiling point.

12. VISIBILITY

"If no one saw you piss in the wind, were you really stupid?"

I WAS ALWAYS ASTOUNDED how often my peers ignored this basic actuality. If your great work or effort wasn't seen, it didn't happen. If you expect your supervisor to devote time studying your daily accomplishments, you will be disappointed.

How do I get noticed without being seen as a major butt munch?

Vignette

Early in my career as a malingerer investigator, I realized the reports I wrote were my only means of visibility. My peer's reports were as short as possible, had no variation in the information, and every conclusion was almost identical. Mine were quite different. Partly from boredom, partly from positive feedback, I tended to go overboard in description and made odd conclusions. While visiting one house, I mentioned they had huge knives and forks on the wall. I wondered if Wilt Chamberlain was coming to dinner that night. On another report, I noted that the malingerer was on the roof repairing tiles and scampered down the ladder like a circus monkey. Perhaps the roof work was a new form of rehabilitation? One disabled guy I interviewed was wearing clothes with every geometric design known to man. Was he trying to hypnotize me with his outfit? One character I investigated was named Brontislav Uzdejczyk. When his parents named him, were they in some alphabet contest? My oddball style got noticed and made the supervisor chuckle. Who do you think got mentioned when a promotion was available?

Visibility Tips:

1. Mimic boss's schedule
2. Play the same sports, hobbies etc. as your manager and discuss them
3. Speak-up in meetings with senior people present
4. Volunteer (only if failure is impossible/unlikely) when the

leader is looking for help

5. Find out what management books they read and mention them casually

6. Make any written material perfect if being read by those above

You get the drift? These are common sense practices but too few people make the effort. There is a belief that "I don't need to stoop to sucking-up because that isn't important anymore." This fallacy will be covered next.

13. SUCKING UP

"Tis an old maxim in the schools'
That flattery's the food of fools:
Yet now and then your men of wit
Will condescend to take a bit."
-Jonathan Swift

WHAT IS THE LESSON HERE? There is almost no bottom line for tasteful sucking-up. Every person you work with is susceptible to flattery. It is hard to suck-up too much. Some people have taken sucking-up to the art level. The only rule is avoiding being so obvious and insincere that you undo your ass kissing. One caveat is the intended object must like you or at least be neutral about you. If the target hates you, avoid them until you find a way to reverse the impression.

Vignette

I worked for Jim near the middle of my career. Jim was a malignant dwarf who did all he could to avoid closeness with his minions. He enjoyed being a prick. Fred was a recently hired peer who seemed to have penetrated Jim's armor. It took me awhile to befriend Fred but we had tennis in common and soon became pals.

"Fred, you're the only one that Jim likes. How did you pull it off? Jim doesn't even seem to like himself."

"During the interview process, I learned where Jim lived and that he was very close and protective with his family. It was clear that he hadn't met many people in the neighborhood and didn't get out much. His wife was getting stir crazy. Since I was relocating anyway, I moved into his neighborhood and made certain my wife went over and introduced herself. Pretty soon, we had my daughter babysitting for them, took them to the airport on family vacations (this avoided cheap Jim paying for parking), picked up their mail while they were away and even took care of the dog. We almost became a butler service but the stock options soften the humiliation. If my lips start to hurt from kissing-up, I buy more Chapstick. I could do this for a few years without any problem."

Fred did all this intentionally. It was part of his plan. He'd done it successfully before. He didn't really like Jim but he loved money. He knew the subservience would pay off. How low are you willing to stoop? Most people won't go this low but Fred had a goal and the money made it worthwhile. Fred was an extreme case and I couldn't have groveled the way he did. However, it's up to you.

14. LOYALTY

"The problem with blind loyalty is you often end up with a seeing-eye dog."

WE ARE TAUGHT IN YOUTH that loyalty is an admirable trait. Being loyal to your family, school, church, friend and team is drummed into us all. In business, loyalty is hardly discussed and rarely demonstrated. With that said, loyalty is always expected. It is just one of those things taken for granted. Like acne in adolescence, it becomes important when least expected and at the most visible moment. There are (2) fundamental loyalty lessons:

Make certain your loyalty is always noticed.

To be noteworthy, you must do something stupendous to warrant recognition. As I said, routine loyalty is like wearing shoes. Make certain you have solid gold kicks on before you start moonwalking. But don't be too obvious as you note the significant act of loyalty. Mention it casually and let other people heap the praise, but make certain your good work is known. Find a balanced way to publicize yourself.

Vignette

Remember my sales boss Mel who had the low boredom threshold? In one high profile sales situation, we failed to write more business with a large client, and Dick, the day to day manager, asked for a formal debriefing to analyze the failure. (Dick was a notorious drunk near the end of his career, mean as a pissant, and he wanted the blame placed anywhere but on him. I worked with this customer, as well, and it was clear they disliked Dick and thought that if Dick was the best we had for them, we must not think much of them.)

Mel and Dick were peers and we all met with the Senior Vice President to review the matter. Dick viciously attacked Mel for being unprepared and not being aggressive enough. Mel didn't want to be viewed as defensive so he listened silently to the rant. I thought I read Mel's dilemma and jumped to his defense.

"We lost the business because they hate your guts, Dick.

You added nothing to the meeting and never showed up for the practice sessions. Point the finger at yourself!"

Dick went postal and we both started shouting at each other. Mel told me to calm down but I could tell he was happy. I was the junior person in the room and was asked to leave by the senior guy. I took a calculated risk that the SVP knew Dick was a boozer and was the true cause of the loss. With that said, I still was queasy as I left.

Dick retired shortly thereafter and I was soon promoted to one of Mel's direct reports. He never thanked me formally but our relationship changed after that day.

Make certain disloyalty is never noticed.

Your career is over if you get caught being disloyal. The boss will get rid of you quickly if open bad-mouthing is proven. Even your competitors will be silently disgusted when you disparage your leader publicly. Your rivals will wonder what you are saying about them if you are so negative about your own leader.

The exception is after a leader has been deposed. I will cover this in a later section. You can be somewhat negative then but it is best to nod your head compassionately and say little.

15. EFFICIENCY

There is no better compliment than to be seen as "efficient." If you are seen as "not only efficient but also effective" it is like winning the Congressional Medal of Honor in business. I saw one career blossom when a woman suggested that office personnel should change the toner cartridge in the copy machine rather than call the Service Company. Everyone changed the toner already but an obscure procedural memo suggested a technician be called. A genius in efficiency was born.

The efficiency craze led to the "Quality" mania that still grips Corporate America. I won't belabor the vagaries of this quality movement but NEVER get into a full-time quality expert job. These are visible and vulnerable (might as well have "shoot me first" written on their chest) positions in bad times. These unfortunates must constantly change processes or their guru status is threatened. Ultimately, somebody will note that the revolutionary, new procedure is the same as the original approach and they're caught.

The trick is consistently finding ways to save the organization money. If a change cuts expense, you got a winner. Make certain the boss knows what you did and let them grab some credit too. Avoid an expectation of creating efficiency changes frequently, just often enough to maintain your reputation.

Vignette

My company was having tough times so they hired Tim as their quality expert. He wrote a groundbreaking book on "insurance quality." At least that's what the publisher said on the jacket cover. I tried to read it but my eyes started to roll back and my hair hurt. The book was unreadable.

Tim was a doctor, lawyer and actuary. This combination of skills was unheard of in our industry. These educational achievements were fiercely neutralized by Tim's lack of common sense, social skills and personal hygiene.

Tim was brought on an important sales meeting and waxed erudite on insurance quality. The clients started showing the same symptoms I had reading his book but they listened politely. After the meeting wrapped up, the customer called me aside and said, "If Tim is your quality guru, how come he can't wear matching shoes?"

I chuckled and rolled my eyes. Tim wandered into the sunset later that year. I think he consults with the North Koreans on their nuclear program.

16. READING THE STREET

HOW ARE YOUR ABILITIES to read your environment? I am always amazed by how clueless people can act. Many wander this earth with no awareness of what goes on around them. Go to the mall and watch people pushing monster-truck baby strollers into tiny, crowded elevators, chatting on cell phones while actively engaged in the restroom or walking semi-nude in the dressing rooms to see proof.

A heightened sense of awareness is a huge advantage in business. Perhaps my early tenure describing the myriad forms of malingering sharpened my skill? For whatever reason, I was very aware of the office dynamics. I spent a lot of time watching what went on around me. Body language tells a story. I observed physical reactions intently. Negative responses sing loudly. How often do you talk rather than watch? Listed below are things to watch for:

1. Watch to see if the boss is distracted.
2. Find out the cause of the problem.
3. Find a tactful way to help the boss.
4. Never present important issues to a boss who is under stress.
5. Does the manager dislike certain peers?
6. Does the boss have favorites?
7. Befriend the favorites.

Back away if you sense a "no" coming to your business request. Analyze the "no" and rephrase for a better outcome.

Vignette

Will was veteran manager in the Blustery City. He was a volunteer fireman and was nuts about fires. He actually kept a fire scanner in his office so he could monitor local disasters. Will never answered his phone if there was a juicy blaze going on. There were rumors that he even left the office if the fire was close by. Do I need to say that this was inappropriate behavior?

Will wasn't our worst manager (other stories will allow you to decide) and I liked him. I warned him that our Regional Director was paying him a "surprise visit" and to curb his pyromania. The RVP showed up next day and popped in on Will. They had a long chat and all went well. The RVP said he was going to visit some other people in the building and wouldn't see him anymore that day.

Will immediately pulled the scanner from its hiding place and flipped it on for the latest horror update. Great news! A fierce blaze was wreaking havoc nearby. Will slammed on his hardhat and catapulted from the office like a deranged banshee. Naturally, this was witnessed by the RVP who had never left the office floor. Will "retired" a couple months later. Despite my warning, Will was unable to adjust his behavior to a different environment. He would be hanging from the ladder truck right now if he altered his habits for one lousy day.

17. TEAM PLAYER

THERE IS A FINE LINE between visibility and being seen as someone who "grabs all the credit." At low to middle career levels, most tasks are team efforts. Praise your teammates publicly and laud the team for any success. Your peers will love the accolades and flock to work with you. Your reputation as a team player will spread like bull-manure at a class reunion. Being a member of a high performing team leads to each individual getting recognized as "a winner."

Note: I didn't do this in a calculated manner. Teamwork is fun and rewarding. It was natural for me. If it isn't for you, work at it.

Most teams comprise of peers from your department or perhaps other organizations. If the task has likelihood for success and visibility, try to get a leadership position. You should do this without being a crazed loon like you see on

"The Apprentice." Most teams are peopled with those who love their defined role or niche. They are content just being part of the action. Size-up those rivals who also want leadership and see if they are talented and true competitors. If they are, find an amicable way to share responsibility. Teams get dysfunctional fast if there is a long squabble for leadership. If the competitor refuses to share leadership, and you think you will win, offer to put the leadership to a team vote. If you think you will lose, graciously accede leadership and revel in the team success.

Vignette

Earlier in this book, I mentioned that the corporate message changes yearly. One year, I was asked to be on a Human Resource team that I knew was a loser. Our job was to convince managers that, during the annual performance reviews, all/most employees should be ranked as "meeting position requirements" and no one "exceeding position requirements."

Historically, managers gave high rankings so they could avoid confrontations. (Behind their backs, the manager would glibly hammer the poor performers.) My dilemma was participating as a good teammate but not getting caught in the inevitable flack and certain reversal of this unpopular review policy.

I suggested to the team that we create another rating level below "meeting position requirements" so employees wouldn't think they got downgraded. In essence, we would make "meeting position requirements" seem more difficult and challenging to achieve. Hence the legendary "frequently meets position requirement" was born. Senior management got their wish, managers got wiggle room and the new HR forms lasted for (3) years before a consultant mentioned the idiocy. I was far gone by then.

18. WORKING WITH THE OPPOSITE SEX

My advice is to treat your co-worker as either Mother Theresa or Pope John Paul. Years ago you could make off-color jokes or innuendo and only get your hand slapped or some stern warning. Today you will get sued, your employer will get sued, and you could lose your job and end up in the newspapers. Even if the joke/wisecrack is borderline, you are tainted by "poor judgement" for putting yourself in a bad situation. There is no win here.

Despite this strict litigious environment, lots of poor behavior still occurs today. Men get lulled into thinking their female workers are "one of the guys" and slip into locker room humor. Don't make this mistake. Most people (male or female) are uncomfortable if sexual topics arise and may listen without complaint but are silently annoyed. Most times nothing happens. Sometime a formal complaint will result and you lose.

We all like humor and wit but stay away from sex jokes. Even at happy hours, you are considered "at work." This may sound too preachy and not in line with my other warped-humor comments, but the advice is solid. If in doubt, be boring at work and save the Mr. Naughty routines for your close friends.

Vignette

Fred was one of the most talented salesmen I had. He was terrific with customers, a creative negotiator and a whiz with numbers. Fred was very popular with his peers and truly a "life of the party" personality. He was also a bit of a chauvinist but his female peers enjoyed him and overlooked his flaws.

Then one happy hour soiree went too long and the group started a game of "what is your dream job?" When Fred's turn came he said, "I want to drive a mobile mammography van so I can keep all you gals pert and perky." There were lots of chuckles and the night ended shortly thereafter. No one voiced displeasure to Fred. What a funny guy, right?

Next morning, I got a formal complaint from HR. I

wasn't present so I had to investigate the allegations. Fred admitted everything and saw no issue with his comments. "Everyone laughed", was his defense. Fred did not lose his job over that single incident but it was one of too many mishaps that caused us to "encourage" Fred to leave the company.

19. PERSONAL HABITS

THIS SOUNDS TOO OBVIOUS to mention, doesn't it? More people lose promotions and remain lifetime middle managers because of annoying personal habits. Worse yet, are disgusting personal habits. I've seen men and women publicly scratching bodily orifices that would give porno stars pause. Then you start thinking about why they need to scratch and it deteriorates from there.

This is the simplest section of this tome. Come to work clean, groomed and act like it's your first date with the girl/boy of your dreams. It isn't vital that you make a great impression. It is vital that you avoid the dreadful impression. You don't want people talking at the water cooler about your quirks. With little effort, you can be neutral.

Vignette

Kevin was a down-home, fun-loving guy I worked with in the Midwest. He was also a world-class slob who did something weekly to gross-out people. Kevin smoked like a fiend and held his cigarette upside down to keep the ash stacked-up as long as possible. You always hated to see him near the end of his smoke. Somehow that precarious ash pile would land on your pants or desk. It gets worse.

We were meeting with our largest customer to resolve some significant service problems. Kevin was responsible for customer relations and had a great rapport with the unhappy customer--but they had never met live. All interactions were by telephone. Kevin was introduced and went about explaining what the action plans were to fix the concerns. Midway through his discussion, Kevin leaned down from the table and literally removed his right shoe. Without missing a syllable with the customer, Kevin looked deep into the shoe and started shaking it. Then he removed a sock and shook that too. Apparently satisfied with his housecleaning, Kevin redressed and concluded his speech.

The customer sat there without saying anything and Kevin left when he was done explaining his plan. We preceded to wrap-up other financial matters and the meeting ended cordially.

Before they left, the senior customer rep quipped, "I thought Kevin was doing an Agent Maxwell Smart imitation and was making a call on his secret shoe phone."

I smiled and apologized for the unplanned entertainment. Kevin lasted for many years but never progressed beyond middle management. He's probably balancing an ash as we speak.

SECTION 2

MIDDLE MANAGEMENT

20. DRIVE

DON'T CONFUSE DRIVE WITH AMBITION, aggressiveness and competitiveness. People with drive have a fire in their belly. They have great ambition and competitiveness but they also have the ability to focus all their energy towards completing major goals. A driven individual likes the process of getting over the goal line and won't be distracted by setbacks. The act of achieving or acquiring their aim is as important and gratifying as the actual result.

Drive can overcome lack of talent or natural advantages. Many CEO's come from small colleges and are introverted. None of the best senior leaders I encountered had overwhelming innate gifts. All the great ones had drive. Once these leaders locked on a purpose, they got it done.

How do you know if you have drive? It isn't that easy to gauge. I once went to a sales "charm school" with the "best and brightest" in that corporation. There was an extremely aggressive guy (Pat) who dominated any discussion. One drill was for each class member to identify your style out loud. When they got to Pat he said, "I'm a driver, driver." When they got to me I said," If Pat's a driver, driver then I'm a passenger, passenger." Everyone laughed but I wasn't joking entirely. Pat was far more aggressive than I would ever be. However, he wasn't more driven than I was.

Vignette

Sue was a fast tracker who I was assigned to mentor. She was in the Finance Department and judged to be a future leader. I called Sue's boss to get more background and heard glowing details of her skills and potential. Just as we were concluding, the boss said, "There is one thing about Sue that bothers me but I can't put my finger on it." I asked more questions but got nowhere. (Many Finance people aren't articulate. Too busy with the beans.)

I met with Sue and saw all the skills and potential but also noted she was very dissatisfied. Nothing seemed to move quickly enough or come out as she wanted. Because of his packed schedule, she could never get enough time with the boss to air her views. I gave her many suggestions about staying late and getting more face time with her boss after normal business hours.

After a few months of the same complaints, I asked whether she had any luck getting more visibility. Sue told me, "I spend too much time at work as it is. I'm in a bowling league and that starts at 5pm. Bowling is my passion. Mom said I was born to bowl."

Sue never progressed beyond lower level assignments but her bowling average topped 200 one year. The only drive she had was in her bowling ball release.

21. DISPARAGING THE COMPETITION

"There is always a spitball poised and ready to be launched at you."

I KNOW THIS SOUNDS TERRIBLE. Surely we can take the high road and rest on our laurels as self-evident proof of our superiority? It doesn't work that way. Not everybody plays fairly. I'm not suggesting any vicious, inaccurate smear campaign. I'm suggesting that you trumpet your successes and find a way to kick a little dirt on your competitor. If you had the covert opportunity to check, you would find some mud coming your way from a rival's boots.

You can rarely win this type of contest by pure negatives. You need clear, positive results on your side or the snipping will be obvious. Lead with strength before you attack the weakness. Try to be subtle and make sure your negative facts are right. Determine if your rival has enemies and gain their help. The wolf pack is tougher than the lone wolf. If you don't have the stomach for the fight, be satisfied with where you are.

Vignette

Dick Byrne and I were vying for a key sales position. Dick had more experience, had an MBA and spent lots of time networking. He was also a bit pompous and wasn't the hardest worker. I heard one senior leader make a comment that Dick had "Champagne taste but beer input." Unfortunately, this leader wasn't involved in the decision but it gave me an idea.

A large meeting of our unit was ending and our boss and others (Dick Byrne included) were shooting the breeze. During a pause I said to Dick, "You know, when I first met you I wasn't sure if Dick Byrne was your name or a painful diagnosis."

The room was all males and the quip got big laughs and was repeated for many years. Dick had no good comeback, got red in the face and huffed out of the room. I got the promotion and Dick ended up working for me. He really was lazy. He didn't last long.

22. HELPING PEERS TO SUCCEED

THIS MAY SEEM CONTRADICTORY with the disparaging competitor advice. It isn't. Most co-workers are not rivals for the same promotions. You should assess who are the most talented peers from other departments and gain their confidence. Many of these people will rise with you throughout your career and can be important allies. Corporations are bureaucratic and opinionated. Most key corporate projects get wide organizational attention and involvement and can't succeed if negatives surface broadly from other units.

Many segments of corporations are highly technical and the prominent young leaders aren't that savvy on these chameleon skills. Look for opportunities to help these "techies" to get ahead. Mention ways for them to get noticed and they will be forever grateful. Something that is obvious to you would never occur to them. Simple things like dress, grooming or annoying habits might go forever unnoticed but remain forever a career roadblock. Look for quirks and help them.

Vignette

Lloyd was an actuary who came into the company at the same time I did. He was a brilliant mathematician and a great guy .He knew he was "out there" a bit but his raw ability got him by. We played on the same company basketball team and became good friends. We were as different as night and day but the friendship worked.

My career was blossoming and Lloyd seemed stuck. He asked for advice and I did a little digging with the leaders of his department. About all I could find as negatives were "weird mannerisms" that weren't viewed as "officer material." I got this quirk narrowed further and met with Lloyd. "Lloyd, do you know that you have a tendency to "deep breathe" when you are having conversations with people?"

Lloyd replied that he learned in a Zen book to take "10 deep breathes when in stressful situations." He added that he found the technique had broader application and allowed him "to concentrate and focus more."

"Lloyd, that might allow you to focus more but the people you're with think you're either nuts or having a seizure. Stop the Zen crap and your boss won't worry about putting you out in public." He looked at me funny but said "I never thought about that." Lloyd stopped the hyperventilation and had a great career. He is still odd but lovable.

23. THE POWER OF QUESTIONS

ONE OF THE CLEVEREST VERBAL TOOLS I learned was asking questions. One of my closest friends used questions like a saber and I stole her approach for work. There are many applications for the technique. You will hear many stupid things in your worklife and rather than flatly say "Hey, moron, that is the dumbest idea in history", you can ask "Tell me why you think that will work?" Many times when you get people to talk their brilliant idea through, they see the lunacy.

Another value from questions is forcing people to clarify their thoughts. Even good ideas often come too weak on details. Asking questions will get the thinker to list the values and also prompt loose ends to be identified. Once the positives are compiled, the facts may be compelling enough to act on. It is easy to miss great suggestions when they came to you without enough meat. Questions put meat on the bones.

Don't overdo this interrogatory approach or you may lapse into the "answering a question with a question" pit. If you see that "why this and why that" is frustrating the person (and they are a subordinate), then be direct that you have doubts about their idea and shut them down. If you employ this interrogatory technique with superiors and they get annoyed, then stop and wait for a better moment to voice your concerns. No one likes pesky minions. Use the suggestions in Positive Approach (Chapter 6 in previous section) to get yourself through this morass.

Vignette

"If cleanliness is next to godliness, can a pig get to heaven?"

How people come dressed for work is a subject of immense management interest. If the corporation is having a poor quarter or missed key objectives, someone will blame "poor dress and the resultant lack of professionalism" as the cause. Slovenly people better guard their loins because a new dress code is coming hard.

In such an environment, I was asked to participate as a senior sponsor for a project team asked to redefine the corporate dress standards. HR people tend to lead these tasks and this group was no exception. The early brainstorm sessions were classic sartorial bashing. A sub-team was asked to do the first draft of a new code and the following litany of unacceptable dress resulted.

Attire Not Acceptable:

1) Jeans and denim wear-- including all denim of various colors. (This was a stroke of genius to prevent creative flouting of the rules. Radicals might try to slip non-blue color denim past the fashion police.)

2) Corduroy (fine or large groove) is forbidden. "Brushed" corduroy will fall into the fine groove definition and is similarly banned.

3) Casual/beachwear outfits to include shorts, capris pants (a.k.a. peddle- pushers), skorts (culottes fit in this category), sundresses and any article resulting in a bare midriff.

4) Tank tops, halters or inappropriately tight tops that is "suggestive or sexy."

5) Any clothing with obscene, lewd or inappropriate sayings or logos.

You get the idea. With a serious face I asked this team the following:

"Do you think our supervisors could distinguish between finely brushed corduroy and acceptable worsted wool?"
"Why have you left the door open for halter tops that offer no suggestion of sexiness?"
"Why have you limited the nudity ban to midriffs? Don't we need to make certain that absolutely no organs are visible?"

Not one committee member laughed or got my humor. They did get so distracted by how huge the no-no list could be that we never got anywhere. The next quarter was hugely successful and our project team disbanded from lack of interest.

24. MOTIVATION

"If you beat people senseless, they become senseless."

I GREW UP WITH FOOTBALL coach Vince Lombardi as the model of coaching and motivation. Treat everyone the same-like dogs. Push people, be harsh, never be satisfied and always raise the bar. I was foolish like many young managers and swallowed this swill.

What I learned was that no single management approach lasted too long. You had to change to circumstances and people. Sometime you pushed and sometime you encouraged. Praise didn't last any longer than criticism. You had to stay alert to how the style was working. Modify the approach if stagnation occurred.

The most successful technique was the "60% rule." The top "20%" need no motivation and the bottom "20%"

wouldn't listen to Noah if he sailed by on the Arc. Focus on that middle "60%" to carry the show. How you get this large, self-contented group moving sharply will control your destiny.

One mistake I made as a young manager was setting goals that were overly aggressive and challenging. I set the target so high that this 60 % couldn't meet it consistently. They went home each night thinking they failed. Who likes being a failure? The middle roader wants to feel like a winner.

I soon started to set realistic goals that were marginally higher and praised the people daily. If they slipped sometimes, I remained enthusiastic and supportive. I told my team that everyone has an off day. Gradually, the numbers in the office got better. Each quarter showed steady improvement and year end showed great progress. I was a hero.

Inevitably results would stall and new "moves" were required. Occasionally, I acted "disappointed" if results sagged. Since workers are expecting to be "yelled at", they are often momentarily sympathetic for the boss and results tick-up. Don't use this disappointment routine too often. You can quickly lapse into the wimpy boss arena.

The rule is to treat the "60%" with mostly positive stroking. You have to be persistent, visible and a cheerleader. Don't be discouraged by small setbacks. If you stay the course, this powerful mass of people will relentlessly move forward.

Vignette

I read a book about empowering your management team. The theory was to give your supervisors clear responsibility for specific goals, then sit back and enjoy the fruits of your wisdom. As a newer manager, I believed much of what I read. If someone got a book published, how could they be stupid? Wouldn't that be a nasty prank? I accepted what I read and acted on the advice.

I dutifully met with my supervisors, set challenging goals and told them I would check a week later to gauge progress. I made myself unavailable and gave no advice or suggestions. A week later, we assembled and reviewed the numbers. They were horrible. Everything went backwards. I kept my cool and again told them they "were in charge and to make decisions like it was their company."

Another week went along and the results were worse than ever. My anger showed and I told them they failed. "I'LL GIVE YOU ONE MORE WEEK AND YOU BETTER TURN THIS AROUND."

Again, I remained aloof and was convinced they got the message. My grand empowerment would save the day. I got the numbers before the formal meeting and everything was worse than ever. Didn't these knuckleheads see my benevolence for giving them control?

I talked to my very sage wife and told her I was writing "final warnings" on the supervisors and would deliver them at the Monday meeting.

"Do you really think that group has the ability to run the operation? Based on what I see, there aren't too many sharp pencils in that case." Her comments stopped me cold. I had to admit my supervisors were marginal and would never rise higher. I looked at her. "I hate it when you're so damned right."

The 60% rule fits for management levels as well. If you have marginal leaders, they need the same style of treatment as line workers. I went in that Monday and told them my mad experiment was over and that we needed to work together to get the ship turned. They were visibly relieved, listened to what I needed done and did it. Nothing happened quickly but all the metrics improved steadily. I praised, cajoled and cheered them back to success. A painful lesson but one I never forgot.

25. WRITTEN COMMUNICATION

"I ain't kiddin ya, people don't write good."

WRITING IS A LOST ART IN BUSINESS. I've listened to many leaders who spoke well but could never capture their passion or clarity in writing. What they said was vastly different when it fell to paper. The message was either too wordy or too vague. Verbal people tend to be the worst writers. If you pointed out the obtuseness, the high verbal often got defensive. "You know what I meant. Just do what I said," was the retort.

It was true that some might know exactly what the speaker meant, but anyone that hadn't heard the speaker live, or paid close attention, often relied on the follow-up memo. Then the mischief started. Readers would always interpret to the least amount of work or assume others were accountable.

"Oh, you wanted me to do that project? Can you show me that in the memo?" became an art form response to the canny work shirker.

Acronyms and abbreviations are the crutch of the writing impaired. I worked for Mike Van Derkamp when I was a wily young supervisor. Mike abbreviated everything and always signed his name "Mr. V.D." Needless to say, everyone laughed when they saw his memos and forgot what he asked to be done. Couldn't be too important if it came from Mr.Veneral Disease, could it?

Be short and sweet when you write business notes. State the problem or task in the beginning and ask for a specific outcome. Set clear dates when you need something completed and ask to be called if the goal needs to be clarified. Always follow-up with telephone calls if the matter is critical or urgent. The more you write, the more wiggle room you allow. Discipline yourself to be concise.

Ask a friend who writes well to give you candid feedback. If you don't see improvement, enroll in a business writing course. These courses tend to be more elaborate than necessary but you will learn techniques for clarity. Writing is a skill that practice can make better, if not perfect.

Vignette

Years ago, I worked in an office with an automated mail cart. This robotic cart followed a track around each floor and stopped at designated locations. Each of us was responsible to get our mail as the cart stopped near our workspace. Much of the mail was attached to a "routing slip" that listed many names. Your job was to read the mail then route it to the next name on the slip. Most of the stuff was useless but the workers read everything diligently if it had a routing slip.

As an experiment (and for my amusement), I started routing odd things on the mail cart. With a few friends watching my folly, I successfully routed the Burpee Seed Catalogue, The Yellow Pages and a TV repair manual around the whole floor. I noted on the routing slip that they should "Please read carefully and send to the next listed worker promptly." and then watched people snag the bulky material. I got the pointless stuff back, since I was the last name on the routing slip. Every time!

I realized that this was immature and frivolous. It did teach me that specific and concise writing could be powerful. If the instructions were clear and official, you could make the masses respond to almost anything. Fortunately, we had no bridges on my floor to tempt me.

26. PUBLIC SPEAKING

WE ALL KNOW THAT PUBLIC SPEAKING is the greatest personal fear. I was no different from anyone else. Most of my formative years were filled with witty one-word responses. As a product of Catholic schools, I was taught to raise my hand and wait to be called on before answering a question. If you played it right, someone always beat you to the punch. My hand was always a tad slow.

I was never forced to say much until I got to the business world. Like my peers, I struggled through my initial speaking roles. Unlike most of my peers, I was not content to be a mumbling buffoon. Surely, I could do better than this. Was I condemned to be inarticulate?

Speaking effectively in small, informal office meetings and large group presentations in formal settings was a major asset to your career. Rather than accept that I couldn't get better, I went to work. I read a few public speaking books and got some good suggestions. Most of the precepts in these self-help tomes were similar, so I won't recommend a specific one. Go to the bookstore and look for the current latest and greatest. What I found and did is listed below:

1. If you want to be a better speaker, you can be.
2. You can be a very good public speaker, even if terrified.
3. You don't need natural ability to get good.
4. The more you practice, the better you get.
5. Practice in small meetings to build confidence.
6. Join Toast Masters to hone your nerve.
7. Practice out loud.
8. Memorize the speech but make it sound conversational.
9. Many great speakers are introverts.
10. Add humor- even if you aren't a funny type.
11. Shorter is better than longer. People bore easily.
12. Set realistic expectations. Good is all you need to be.
13. Keep spinach and peppercorns out of your teeth.

Vignette

Joe and Ted were peers who co-managed a small business unit. It is awkward to have two leaders but this compromise happened during a merger of two firms. They worked well together but were dramatically different styles. Ted was verbal, gregarious and comfortable leading. Joe was cerebral, an expert technician but as nervous as Madonna at a Mensa meeting.

At the first gathering of leaders from the combined firms, we were all required to address the group to explain our plans and goals. Ted went first and did a great job. He explained his half of the combined unit, was funny, and hit all the key points. Perhaps he was too wordy but he'll read this book and expect a jab.

Then came Joe. A small guy anyway, he came to the podium and never adjusted the microphone lower. Try to picture Joe's head barely over the podium with his eyes looking skyward. As he muttered nervously, Joe realized he couldn't be heard. When he tried to adjust the mike, he hit the button that raised the podium upward. Then you couldn't see Joe at all. People started to chuckle.

Joe panicked and stopped talking. He kept playing with the podium and couldn't get it right. At different points, Joe looked gigantic and then invisible. Then he froze for what seemed like forever before walking off the stage. He never completed his speech and soon became Ted's underling.

27. VOICE MAIL

VOICE MAIL CAN BE AN EFFICIENT way to communicate. It can also be the worst way to communicate if abused. Most people struggle to optimize this electronic timesaver. Listed below are the rules I used religiously:

1. If the message is really important, call the person "live."
2. If you send an important v-mail, listen to what you said before sending it. Check for voice tone, clarity, and grammar.
3. Make certain your message is clear and crisp. People tune-out fast.
4. Restate the crux of the message at least twice.
5. Never respond to an annoying v-mail when you are angry.
6. Call them or delay response until you are calmer.
7. If you did something noteworthy (major sale etc.), copy-in senior leaders to your modest description of the

accomplishment.

8.Never send profanity or sensitive personal issues over v-mail.

Vignette

Louie was born to sell. He loved people, was a world-class schmoozer and sucked–up to superiors like they were God's second son. I asked Louie to host a customer event for me when I was double-booked. That was where Louie met Glenna, our corporate event planner. I got great reports from Glenna about Louie's performance and the customers all seemed to enjoy themselves.

Shortly thereafter, I asked Louie to transfer to the West Coast. A few days later I picked up my voice mails and was puzzled to find a seductive, sultry love message from Louie. The gist of the message included what circus tricks that "Monty the love snake" could perform. Toward the close, Louie mentioned my request to transfer and how this might ruin their wild monkey love. I vaguely caught Glenna's name at the close.

Glenna and I had a similar beginning to our last names. Louie had put Glenna and me on his voice mail abbreviation list and sent me the soft porn call by accident.

I called Louie and told him "if he talked dirty to me anymore the transfer was off." I explained his mistake and ended the call with "does this mean you don't love me anymore?" The horny couple did marry and Louie had a great career on the Left Coast. He was lucky I had a twisted side.

28. E-MAIL

ALL THE TECHNIQUES I MENTIONED earlier in the section "Written Communication," applies here. Since most written business communication comes by e-mail, here are a few specific suggestions to maximize the written word.

1. Never send profanity by e-mail. Even funny ones.

2. Never log onto pornographic web sites at work. Even good ones.

3. Don't send e-mails with zillions of attachments.

4. Don't pass e-mails that have an endless string of useless comments.

5. If passing to your boss, summarize long e-mails upfront and make recommendations.

6. Don't bitch-out people over e-mail. This leaves an audit trail for anyone with an attorney and an axe to grind. (Bitching-out is more fun in person, anyway.)

Most of this is common sense but that trait is rare in the business world. Many business gnomes use e-mail to effectively avoid accountability. "Let me show you this email. I can prove that I never agreed with anything" is a familiar refrain. The best of these connivers have huge databases that confirm that they never took a clear position on any issue in their business life.

Vignette

Big companies have people working 24/7 to find workers that abuse e-mail. Besides writing this book, that job always appealed to me as a fun retirement option. I digress. I was managing a large operation in the South when I got a call from the corporate spooks. One of my managers was routing the following e-mail and they wanted his head.

The Italian who came to Chicago

Ima don lak Chicago worth a sheet. I check inna hotel an go down for breakfast an I tella da girl I wanna hame & eggs an two peese toast, she bringa me hame & eggs and one peese toast. I tella her I wanna two peese, she say ifa you wanna peese, go to da toilet. I say don unnerstan. I wanna to peese on my plate. She say don peese on your plate you sonna ma beech. I never see dat lady before inna my life, and she call me a sonna ma beech. I don eat, I go to my room.

At luncha time I go donna da street for my lunch inna da Drake Hotel. The waitress she brings me a knife and napkin but na fok. I tell her I wanna fok. She say what you talk, everyone wanna fok. I say you no unnerstan, I wanna fok on da table, she say you no care where you fok, you sonna ma beech. So when she call me a sonna beech, I go back to da hotel. When I get inna room, Ima got no sheet on my bed, so I calla da manager an tella him I wanna sheet on my bed. He say donna sheet on you bed, go to da bathroom. Ima say you no unnerstan, I wanna sheet on my bed. He say you better not sheet ona you bed you sonna ma beech. So when he calla me a sonna ma beech, I go to check out. Ima go to da desk to check out to New York, and when Ima leave, the manager say, peace on you. I say peese on you too, you sonna ma beech caus Ima go back to Italy.

Does culturally insensitive pop into mind? After stifling a chuckle, I assured Inspector Clouseau that I would reprimand the offender and make certain that decorum was restored. When I spoke to the joker, I told him this anecdote was funny to some people but offensive to many and was inappropriate at the workplace. I did keep a straight face and he never knew I kept his artwork. This is fairly tame stuff in the real world but corporate America is devoid of humor. I have much juicier examples but the censors wouldn't let me use them.

29. LEADERSHIP

"You can put a tuxedo on a turd, but it remains a turd."

NO BIG NEWS HERE- people are born with natural leadership ability. If you aren't one of the lucky ones, there aren't any magic books or courses you can take to become an inspiring leader. Don't despair. Even if you have no natural leadership skills, you can offset this gap by organizational talent, meticulous business planning, strong communication, strength of will and effective delegation.

If you are appointed to lead a key project (and know you lack charisma), you should look for team members that are natural leaders and use them to accomplish key parts of a project. Praise these minions and use them shamelessly to accomplish the goal. Maybe you never get accolades as "dynamic" but you get a reputation as "someone that gets things done." Results are better than charm.

The best leaders I met were people with great common sense. They anticipate well and plan for outcomes before their competitors know what hit them. The best leaders handle adversity calmly and don't overreact rapidly. They think before they act. Many people confuse loud, glitzy reactions to failure as "being decisive." More often than not, they were decisively stupid.

What I learned was natural leaders weren't always successful. If they didn't possess other business attributes (smarts, discipline, technical acumen etc.), they failed. It might be a glorious, flamboyant failure, but it remained a dud when the dust settled. I liked working for ego-less scrappers. These leaders fought for each inch and willed success with relentlessness.

Vignette

Steve was the least likely natural leader you ever saw. He was short, bald and had yak-like breath. Steve offset these challenges by relentless weight lifting, inexorable will, brilliant thinking, driven work ethic and a great sense of humor. He inherited a management team, during a merger, which was socially and mentally challenged. This team ranged from young superstar to old war-horse.

Steve took some time to assess the team of miscreants and tried something unique to create team chemistry. He trucked us to an off-site survival camp in the Vermont mountains- in the winter! All activities were outside in the freezing cold. All involved team challenges. Everyone had to complete the task or all failed. The young and athletic had to help the linebacker sized codgers over balance beams and through labyrinthine obstacles.

Each night the team was tired and pissed. Steve showed sympathy by having a forced march each night through the frigid town. Smoking cigars was mandatory-even the women. Steve said he didn't want to be the only one with mule breath. Then we adjourned to drink beer and each of us had to talk about ourselves.

One night, a young misfortunate made the mistake of saying, "people say I look like Rob Lowe." Steve looked at the young buck and said, "You look more like Pee Wee Herman to me."

We all belly-laughed at the poor jerk. By the end of the week this team of misfits started working together. We galvanized around our desire to avoid Steve's barbs. For some reason we liked Steve but no one knew why. Kind of like that irritating back pain you get used to. Steve was not a natural leader but he was extremely creative and effective. He found a way to herd the swine.

30. MEETINGS

MEETINGS SHOULD BE CONVENED when you need to:

1. Communicate new information
2. Brainstorm for ideas
3. Discuss/finalize major ideas
4. Clarify goals
5. Finalize decisions

These meetings should include accountable workers with a common goal. When done effectively, meetings are of critical value to a well-run company. When abused or mishandled, meetings are a disastrous drain to company productivity.

This section is divided into "useless" and "useful" meetings, then concludes with how to run meetings effectively. It takes practice and experience determining which category of meeting lurks around the corner. You'll know when you picked poorly.

Useless Meetings

Corporate America wastes more time in bad meetings than Crisco does on fat-in-the-can jokes. Strong companies meet judiciously and make certain they are decision-oriented gatherings. Even great companies have lapses and need to stay vigilant. A friend of mine just entered the corporate world after being self-employed for over thirty years. "You can't freakin' believe how many meetings we have" he said recently. Oh yes I can!

Avoiding meetings is a developed skill. If you know (or are uncertain) that a proposed meeting is a clunker, follow these tips:

1. Never agree to meetings quickly. Always say, "Let me check my calendar and I'll get back to you."
2. Make certain you see who has accepted and judge if you need to attend. Go if your boss is there.
3. Don't go if no important people are there.
4. Decline the invitation with "I'm already booked then."
5. Wait until the last minute before declining.
6. Offer an alternative time that you are certain no one will like (Friday afternoon)
7. Manage your own calendar closely. If you have an administrator, make certain you review with him/her before

agreeing to meet with certain people. (Discuss list of losers beforehand with administrator.)

8. Become ill as a last resort. Something vile, repugnant and contagious.

Useful Meetings

1. It is usually clear if a meeting is important. Look for the following signs to determine relevance:
2. Senior leaders are attending
3. Key initiatives from your business plan are being discussed
4. Decisions are an expected outcome
5. Action items are being produced for senior management and will be monitored.

If you are attending, make certain you read the material and are involved in the discussions! If unable to prepare thoroughly, cram some of the material and speak early in the session on the topic you crammed. You will create the impression of knowing the material thoroughly. Catch up later.

Meeting Management

There is art to running good meetings. After attending lousy meetings, you will quickly note when a maestro has the reins. This is a skill that can be rapidly improved. All you need is willingness, discipline and practice. Here are the winning principles:

1. Keep meetings to (1) hour or less
2. Have an agenda
3. Stay on agenda unless a key issue surfaces that was missed
4. Get people involved. Ask them to comment if they are silent
5. Infuse humor to cut tension
6. Don't allow laptops, Blackberries etc. (people *will* e-mail)
7. Turn off cell phones!
8. Summarize key points out loud and ask for agreement
9. Allow some "discussion drifting" if it adds enthusiasm

Vignette

Our COO went on vacation and read a business book touting the prudence of management staff being located in the center of the floor, in window-less offices. Put the lower level office workers near the windows so they feel important. Human Resources took this wisdom as gospel and started evicting the VP's from their beloved windows. All hell broke loose and I was assigned to mediate "exceptions." I played Solomon and thought we had everyone settled-down. Foolish me.

HR called for "a meeting" to discuss the litany of negative feedback that surfaced from the VP's. I asked to review the list of concerns before meeting with the VP's. Listed below are the items I reviewed with HR:

1. "Why did I put their offices near the restrooms? Was I trying to send some signal?
2. "Don't like the gray leather chairs. Gives the impression of uncertainty. Couldn't they have darker colors? It seems more decisive."
3. "Some offices face the town dump (about (3) miles away and impossible to see except by birds). How did I decide who got the dump view?"
4. "Certain offices have 'white noise' vents and some don't. How did I decide who needed quiet?"

There were other momentous gripes but you get the idea. The HR reps looked at me and I said, "Tell them to pound sand." Since I didn't say anything else, they squirmed around and found nicer ways to phrase my feedback. We then joked about how crazy people can be and adjourned.

If you are puzzled, this was a useless meeting. Each of these VP's could have called me directly and I would have listened to their issues. They knew me well enough that I wasn't patient with trivial issues. They thought that ganging up on me, in a meeting with HR, that I would find some importance in their complaints. Wrong conclusion. Don't let people waste your time.

31. NEGOTIATING

As a young lad, I never appreciated the power of negotiation. Catholic school taught me obedience to my superiors. It took me awhile to see that some superiors were disguised inferiors. Already into my thirties, I learned to love the art of negotiation. Dealing in the gray light of uncertainty was my favorite turf. I got energized when someone said, "This is how it is. It isn't negotiable." Boy, were they foolish.

There are numerous books on improving your negotiating skill. I read many and got value from each. There is always something to learn about how to maximize this ancient skill. Listed below are valuable lessons I learned and practiced relentlessly:

"Win-Win" is the preferable outcome.

You hit a homerun if both parties walked away satisfied. Prior to "live" meetings with the adversary, assess what is really vital then add "nice-to-have" items. Start by asking for the moon but show willingness to discard lesser points. Never let your lesser points seem unimportant.

Many people don't like to negotiate and you will make them feel great if they won any point. Other people will fight like wolverines over minute details. Make your list of lesser points longer with these aggressive characters and be willing to let most of them disappear. Act chagrined with each lost point.

Most people will have their key requirements and that is all they want. If you can assess what those major items are quickly, you will save time. Many people will blurt them out. If your opponent's demands aren't a problem for you, haggle a little, then give them their wish list and walk away the humble victor. This isn't mean or heartless. This is how the world works.

"Lose-Lose" happens sometimes.

There are some issues that can't be resolved or compromised. When you get in this situation, find a way to say that you "agree to disagree." Try to maintain composure and keep the disagreement from getting personal. Once you get passion involved, most conversations go downhill quickly.

If the negotiation is with a customer and deteriorates, try to avoid a clear "no" when you can. I did this frequently by saying, "Based on the new information you gave me today, I need to evaluate this further and get back to you." Most times people will let you off the hook. It is not as difficult or personal to say "no" later, over the telephone.

There are some instances when you must give a final "no" to a demand. If that happens, one technique I used effectively was saying, "Reluctantly, I have to say no. However, I'd like to keep the discussion going and see if we have missed some common ground."

You are sending a message to the other party that you are flexible and want to find a way to make a deal. You are upset that an agreement couldn't be resolved. The lack of a deal wasn't anything personal. This tactful "no" was not a sign of failure for either party.

Vignette

Some people are bad negotiators. If you know that an individual is a poor negotiator, keep them off your team. If you can't avoid them, minimize their roles. I learned this lesson the hard way. We had a challenging renewal with a large customer. I was new to this client and was assigned to retain this important relationship because of my negotiating reputation.

Wayne was an experienced technician on the account but was always a "back room" guy. I needed Wayne to take part in the discussion since he worked with the customer for many years. Wayne seemed thrilled to be involved and did well in the practice sessions. I was puzzled why my predecessor never used him before. He was very likeable and knew everything about the case.

The "live" customer meeting arrived and I started the discussion by waxing eloquent about the value of their business and explained that Wayne would outline the numerous value-added services we provided. (The plan was that after hearing this impressive litany, the customer would clearly see that our fees were justified!)

Like any good presenter, I made eye contact with the customer during my introduction and when I turned to introduce Wayne, I noticed he had his head on his forearms, almost touching the table.

"And now Wayne will go through our services." No answer from Wayne. He seemed almost asleep.

I raised my voice louder and said, "Wayne, you're up." Still nothing from Wayne. Almost yelling, I said "Wayne!!!"

He looked up and said, "HUH?"

"You need to explain the services to our customer."

"HUH?"

I apologized to the customer and asked if we could take a quick break. Wayne was frozen with stage fright. I returned to the room and told the customer that Wayne was ill. I knew enough to wing his part and we retained the customer. Fortunately, this customer did not enjoy negotiating. I think they felt sorry for us and gave us points for not bringing a flashy sales team. We were lucky.

32. KNOWING WHEN TO LOSE

"To everything there is a season… a time to get, a time to lose..."
-Ecclesiastes

THIS IS A DIFFICULT POINT to grasp. We are taught to fight hard and to win at all cost. This conscious plan to lose seems so negative and weak a concept that many never learn it. What I mean is a thoughtful evaluation of your challenge and the mature judgement that you can't win. Failure should be infrequent but by knowing it always happens sometime, you can manage it.

Some of the best leaders I met were experts at losing gracefully. They didn't make a habit of losing, but they handled it with a sense of confidence. They made you think this loss was a bump in the road of a long journey to greater success. You had the feeling they saw how to solve the "real" puzzle. They hated losing but you couldn't tell. Great discipline.

There are business leaders who lost some battles intentionally. They wanted a psychological edge. A more meaningful battle was coming with the same adversary and they wanted some advantage if a prolonged negotiation occurred. They wanted the right to say, "You won that last point, didn't you? You have to give me something."

Give a little to get a lot.

Vignette

I was part of a sale "swat team" sent to write a prestigious piece of business in the western region. We had almost no presence there and were anxious to become a player. Because we were so small, we had no meaningful service infrastructure and our task was to convince the buyer that we could install what they needed in time. Hence the swat team of convincing speakers. However, we knew going in that the incumbent service provider had little to no chance of losing the business. The classic uphill battle.

Leslie was new to our company and was hired because of her expertise in the services we lacked. Leslie knew we had no infrastructure in place and that it would take a miracle to get everything done on time. I started the meeting and told the client how everything would run after Leslie built the structure. The customer peppered me with ultra-detailed questions but I danced like Astaire. I noticed Leslie watched intently.

Leslie got up next and explained her short-term plans, then her vision of where we were headed. She got lathered-up like an evangelical preacher. (I began to worry the customer would start speaking foreign tongues.) She outlined levels of service that I never heard or dreamed of. If the customer wanted the moon, Leslie promised Pluto as well. Just when she said something outrageous, Leslie topped herself in the next statement. The customer seemed amazed.

We left and the lead salesperson stopped Leslie and asked, "What the hell were you doing in there? We will never be able to do what you said. Our credibility will be shot if we fail to deliver."

Leslie said, "I could tell by their questions that they already picked the incumbent. I was just making up ridiculous services to make the incumbent's life unbearable. We'll get another shot in a year or so."

We got the business three years later.

33. THE ART OF GIVING CRITICISM

"How to tell someone they're a horse's ass, but you really like their saddle."

DON'T YOU CRINGE when someone says they want to give you some constructive feedback? Anytime I heard the word "feedback", it made me think about puking. There's nothing constructive about vomit. I always walked away from these sessions as if I was emasculated. It should be called "destructive criticism" to be more accurate.

I'm not unique. Most people take any criticism personally. They react as if you attacked their being. Most of us gauge perfection as some version of ourselves, so mentioning any foible is like a shot in the personals- painfully received and certainly unwelcome. Knowing people will react this way, how can you get the message across without the sensitivity?

De-personalize criticism!

I heard all the time, "I said the same thing you did, but they got pissed off at me. You tell them and they end up thanking you."

If you analyzed the words we both used, you would see differences. The sentences were similar, but I always avoided making it seem that the criticism came from me. I always used "a third person" as having made the comment or observation.

If a person thinks that it isn't "you" saying the negatives, they tend to keep listening. You are just letting them know what is being said or observed by others. You are giving them a chance to debate the criticism without yourself being viewed as the bad guy. If you can keep people talking, you have a chance to convince them that the comments might be inaccurate but "perception is reality."

This sounds easy but it requires preparation. You have to think about the message you want delivered. You have to be direct and clear and yet take the personal sting away from the message. I'm not advocating sugarcoating valid criticism. If there is a real problem, the offender needs to know. Getting them to listen is the skill. Listed below are some phrases I used successfully:

1) A poorly written e-mail needs to be discussed.

"You need to modify this e-mail or people might react negatively. It could be read as very negative. Would you like to discuss ways to get the reaction you want?"

2) The person gave a bad speech.

"I've gotten comments from people that your speech didn't go well. What do you think you could have done differently? Would you like to talk it through?"

3) A middle manager handles a project poorly.

"If you want to become a senior manager, you would need to approach that problem differently. Here is an example of how I've seen that done successfully by a great leader."

4) A new manager handles a personnel matter ineffectively.

"It's not that what you said was wrong, it's how it came across to the listener. Why do you think you didn't get the outcome you wanted?"

I also tried to add something "positive" during the same conversation. For example, even when e-mail is poorly done; there is always something good about it. Don't be obvious about this technique or the person will think you're playing them. Look for something that is truly noteworthy and add that feedback as well.

Example

"Mary, as I told you, that personnel matter didn't go as well as you wanted, but you did a great job analyzing the situation. Most managers wouldn't have detected that portion of the problem at all. Nice work."

This is a skill that you can develop with practice. You will improve quickly if you prepare ahead. After each session, rate how you did. This is harder than "yelling" at your people but the long-term value is immense. Most people never forgive being trashed. Avoid creating enemies when possible. It's not about being popular. It's about being effective and getting results.

Vignette

One of my first opportunities to use this technique involved an immense young woman who worked in my unit. Kim did a good job but I got complaints from her co-workers that "she smelled." The gripes got to the boss and he asked me to have a conversation with Kim.

"Boss, you have to be kidding. You can't tell people they stink. We'll get sued."

"We'll get sued if people pass out at their desk. The girl reeks. Fix it!"

My boss missed that compassion class in school. How could I tell someone they smelled without hurting their feelings? Or getting pounded in the head? It took some time to think of an approach, but here is how it went when I called Kim into a conference room.

"Kim, we need to talk about an aroma that I smell around you. I'm worried that you may have a medical condition that you aren't aware of. Has this medical problem ever happened before?"

Kim was clearly embarrassed but after a moment said, "Now that you mention it, I have had this medical problem before."

I told Kim that it was difficult for people to work around her while this lasted and asked if she could get to the doctor for treatment. "Your co-workers are concerned about you and want to make certain you're okay."

Kim started to bathe regularly again and invested in some deodorant. The stink suddenly disappeared. Nothing like a good doctor to cure what ails you.

34. TAKING CRITICISM

"Sometimes you'd rather have the sharp stick in the eye."

THIS SKILL IS FOR WHEN YOU SIT on the other side of the desk and your boss is giving you some friendly criticism. Most professionals give feedback poorly. They tend to be too obtuse or too harsh. I've walked away from counseling sessions not sure whether I was praised or abused. If you don't know what the boss is saying, stay neutral in your reply and thank them for their time. Try to figure out the message later.

However, you need some real skill for those times when you get direct criticism from your manager. Even if you don't agree with the comments, listen carefully and thank them for their honesty. Tell them "you understand their points and will work to resolve the problem."

Most people start to argue and fume so most managers are pleased and surprised that you took their guidance professionally. I've had some managers apologize to me after taking the comments so well.

It's okay to push back if there was some misunderstanding or if the boss had incorrect information. Restate your view of the facts and see if the leader agrees. If not, don't push it then or you will appear defensive. Let a day go by and schedule some time to review the matter again. Start by saying, "I didn't express myself fully the other day and wanted to make certain you had all the facts." More often than not your boss will judge the issue fairly. Always stay cool.

Vignette

I was one of four people recently promoted to a high-powered sales team. We were expected to "do miracles" and "knock the competition on their tails." (I always remembered to pack a bathing suit when expected to walk on water.) Leading this team was a dynamic salesman who was also a schizophrenic boss. He read management books weekly and changed his style just as often.

Each of us got called in frequently for meetings with the boss and each came out scratching our heads. Sometimes the discussion was motivational and sometime it was a whipping. The most perplexing situation was when all four of us got called in and told, "If I keep seeing the customer complaint logs trending unfavorably, all of you will be fired next week. Now I don't want you to take this as criticism since you are the finest team in the business. I hired each of you personally and couldn't be happier with my choice. I hope this was helpful. Let's get out there and make those customers happy."

We left the room and got far enough away to huddle and compare what we heard. "Were we praised or criticized?"

"Yes" was our joint answer.

This went on for months. We soon began to track when our monthly lashing would occur. Nothing ever happened to us. The boss had read a book on "keeping your troops off balance." I wonder if the book was called "Praise and Confuse?" In case you missed it, this was ineffective criticism. However, the team took the punches like champions.

35. MANAGING OVERWHELMING WORKLOADS

SOME PEOPLE THINK that if they produce mountains of paper, it will prove that they're important. If they also receive volumes of paper, then they're "really" important. Many take pride in complaining that they get hundreds of e-mails and voice mails daily. It's a badge of honor that shouts their value and stature.

"How does this place get by without me", they seem to think.

There is a parallel between a thriving career and workload. The downside with huge workloads is staying on top of it. If you are in the middle of many bouncing business balls then you are expected to make decisions and surface problems. However, if you are always behind, you can get a reputation as "non-responsive." Then people go around you and complain to your boss. Pretty soon you're unemployed and forced to make money selling neck pillows in airports.

How can you keep current with the piles of information and get it all done? It takes discipline and effort. You have to develop routines and not vary from them. Listed below is what I did relentlessly:

Control your work calendar or it will control you

Schedule at least (2) hours daily to read e-mail. Try to make it (2) consecutive hours. I found early morning or around lunch the easiest to manage without interruption. Make certain you don't let "emergencies" interfere with this time. People can be imaginative at defining emergencies.

Scan e-mail

As I mentioned earlier, some people send e-mail to avoid accountability. I learned who these people were and either deleted their messages instantly or sent the e-mail back asking, "What is your recommendation?" I either heard nothing or got a more specific action item. I rarely got junk from the same person after challenging them for clarity.

Create a "general file"

If you scan your work and aren't sure you need to get involved, print it or save to a general file folder. Don't reply to the sender. I looked at this folder every month or so and deleted the oldest month of correspondence if I had heard nothing. I rarely heard from anyone or used the information from this general folder. Somehow, the corporation survived.

Control lunch meetings

Many middle level people use lunch as a time to relax. As your career blossoms, you won't have this luxury. If you aren't using this time to read e-mail, you may need it for networking. What you need to control is people wanting to network with you. You need to decide if there is value from this social contact. Will this person help your cause or a future cause? If the answer is no, make like dynamite and blow them off.

Use voice mail judiciously

I covered this thoroughly in Chapter 8 of this section. However, you need to be selective with voice mail. If you have a reputation as being a selective voice mailer, people will tend to react promptly when you send one. If you shower your co-workers with v-mail, you will generate work for yourself and people may start to ignore you. Then you get backed-up and bad things happen.

Control meeting location

I always assessed beforehand if I was meeting with a highly verbal person. If so, I let them set the location. Even as a senior leader, I rarely had meetings in my office. I was controlling my ability to get up and leave when I wished. If you're in your own office, and not Houdini, how can you leave? If you do get trapped in your office with a motor-mouth, use the "I have another appointment coming shortly" to push them out. Long, unproductive meetings kill your time.

Be direct

We all face situations where we have to ask for something difficult. When in this jam, most people are uncomfortable and avoid blurting out what they want. They do anything to avoid conflict. I'm not advocating being a jackass, just being clear. Tell others what you want and why you need it. If you have a smile on your face, you can say almost anything without being offensive. Don't beat around the bush.

Silence

No response is more powerful than deafening silence. Used selectively, you can say nothing and avoid either reaming someone or getting reamed yourself. If in doubt, shut up. Too many mangers ramble on when they get in an uncomfortable spot. Try being quiet and let your adversary fill in the blanks. Watch them sink their ship.

Vignette

Steve was one of the most talented people I ever worked with. He was a master at managing his schedule. If I was anal, he was flaming anal. One day he was holding a contentious meeting with peers in his office. One of his rivals was ranting about every key issue. Diane was an immensely talented senior leader who enjoyed toying with Steve. Nothing Steve said was "acceptable" to Diane. It was fun watching the jousting.

The meeting was going nowhere and I could see Steve getting are irritated. Suddenly Steve's cell phone went off and he listened intently. He nodded seriously and then stood up and said, "You'll have to excuse me. There's been a possible break-in at my house and I have to meet the police there. I'm not sure how bad this is but I'll need to re-schedule this discussion later."

Steve ran out of the office like enraged Democrats chasing Rush Limbaugh. We all left and even Diane seemed concerned. Later that day I wandered into Steve's office and asked if everything was alright. Steve looked at me seriously but then smiled. "I just faked that because I was about to leap across the table and strangle Diane. I didn't want her to have the satisfaction of making me squirm. I needed time to compose myself."

Steve had his cell rigged to call himself. He varied his "emergency" stories periodically to avoid being predictable. Although admittedly childish, it was a flawless escape plan. This was the perfect way to end an endless meeting. Not a ruse you can use often but I stole Steve's concept more than once.

SECTION 2 SUMMARY

ONCE YOU HAVE MASTERED all the above techniques, you are getting ready to attack the executive level of your career. I asked a Vice President near retirement how he made the VP level. "I knew I was ready when I started to enjoy the taste of bullshit."

I laughed but never forgot the phrase. You need to swallow lots of nasty stuff if you hope to get high on the ladder. Many senior leaders are obviously talented. Others are puzzling choices. I met many high ranking leaders who seemed borderline idiots. How did they get where they were?

I concluded that these baffling senior leaders were very good at something I just covered in this section. And they all had drive. They might be great negotiators but lousy at everything else. However, they parlayed their exceptional skill with immense drive and got where they wanted. Don't underestimate this fact. As you are reading this tome, one of your peers has already decided to make a career move.

SECTION 3

EXECUTIVE SKILL LEVELS

36. CUSTOMER RELATIONS

IT TOOK ME A LONG TIME before I knew I was good with customers. I never realized I had any choice but to treat customers like welcome guests in my home. Weren't these the people that were paying you to provide service? Didn't my paycheck ultimately come from them being happy? Was it an option to treat them like a dirt sandwich?

I learned that most co-workers thought customers were frightening, inanimate objects. Customers were puzzling creatures with some mystical power to maim. Somewhat the same way cavemen looked at Tyrannosaurus Rex. It's okay look hard, but don't screw with them.

I was also attracted to the thought of getting out of the office, having mileage covered and eating great lunches while my mopey peers slaved away. Few of my co-workers liked the customer part of the job and I was viewed as "good with customers." From these humble beginnings, my sales career flourished.

BEST PRACTICES THAT NEVER FAILED

Say their name often

People really love hearing their name out loud. Don't repeat it so often that they think you're a stuttering idiot, but mix it in occasionally. Ask them if you are pronouncing the name correctly. If it's an unusual name (like Bloodlust), ask the origin. If it's an odd name (like Titmouse), act like it isn't. Tell them their name is interesting.

Listen to the customer

Nothing irritates more than someone who doesn't pay attention. Take notes while the customer talks and jot the key points. Just the fact you care enough to note what is said gets you credit.

Acknowledge what was said

When the customer makes a key point, stop them and restate it out loud. Make certain you understand exactly what is expected. Everyone likes hearing that their pearls were fully heard and comprehended.

Avoid disagreement

You might hear that customers don't want "yes men." Yes they do! Do everything possible to agree with what they want. Sometimes you have to disagree but act disappointed that you can't agree. Make it seem that you would concur if it were your choice alone but "that damn boss of mine would never agree."

Determine "hot buttons"

Many customer meetings result in a myriad of demands. Make certain you understand which ones are vital. Then assure the customer that these critical actions will be done on or ahead of schedule. Most customers will allow some minor demands to slip if major tasks get done rapidly.

Summarize action items

As the meeting or discussion is concluding, ask if you can summarize all the takeaways. Tell the customer what items are at risk and get their feedback and agreement on which tasks can be delayed. Ask for due dates on key issues and don't agree if a date is impossible to meet.

Deliver

I've seen incumbents or frontrunners lose many clients because they failed to hit delivery dates. If you know a date is at risk, call the customer and explain the dilemma. Ask if an extension is possible. If yes, make that new date. If the answer is no, move heaven and earth to get it done.

Vignette

John was a "challenging" customer from the Midwest. He had worked previously at my company and left on unfriendly terms. He still liked many of his former co-workers and continued to socialize with them after his departure. I was the new account rep and was assigned to John since he was putting his business out to bid. "An opportunity more than a challenge", I was told. (Don't you love people who can say those lines straight-faced?)

John was a bear of a man with an immense ego. He talked loudly and wanted you to listen and agree. He loved being the customer and made it clear that his important business would come or go on his decision. When I first met at his office, he put his feet on the desk and rocked way back in his chair. He was king and I the humble minion. Even though he had a hole in his shoe.

I called John a few weeks later and discussed some of the terms of our proposal. These had been presented "live" earlier but I was responding to John's follow-up questions. As we got into it, I could hear John recline in his chair and park his clodhoppers on the desk. He wanted to maintain his majesty even over the telephone.

Midway through a sentence, I heard a terrific crash. I waited a bit and kept asking if he was okay. No answer. I heard muffled voices and then the telephone went dead. I was concerned and called back. John's administrator picked up the call and said, "There's been an accident. John can't come to the phone" and she hung up.

I learned through the grapevine that John had fallen ass-over-teakettle from his chair and was knocked unconscious. John was taken to the hospital for treatment of a mild concussion. I learned from his friends that he was very embarrassed by the fall and became even more unbearable.

When I called later to check on the proposal, I never brought the incident up. John was as irascible as ever but we kept the business. He told me later that if I had mentioned the incident to anyone, the case would have moved. He appreciated my discretion. I hope he doesn't read this book!

37. NETWORKING

THERE IS GREAT ART to networking. I was astounded by how often some cohorts talked to peers and superiors just to "keep in touch" or "run an idea by them." This was not my natural style or inclination. I was decisive and didn't tend to chew over tough issues with others. Early in my career, I was taught "a bad decision was better than no decision at all" and to "keep pushing the ball forward." These stupid male sports analogies were okay at lower positions but did not apply at an executive level.

Executives often deal with complex problems. With complex problems, there are lots of diverse opinions. Most executives are smart, have big egos and think they have the best slant on complex solutions. The problem with asking for opinions is that you'll get opinions. Many of these new viewpoints won't agree with what you determined. Then you must tell the "wise one" that you discarded their advice. Your diplomatic skills have to rise to the occasion. Sounds like a lot of work. It is.

Women are far better at networking than men. This isn't a sexist comment. I say this with great admiration. Perhaps because of the "glass ceiling", women were compelled to develop mentors (male and female) and to gain broader support for their decisions than male counterparts. Slowly this unfair situation has improved but women have had it tougher.

The great women leaders I know were more comfortable with gaining input before going too far down the decision road. Women don't seem hung-up with the macho "decisiveness" baggage that plagues the less fair sex. Gaining input is wise not weak. The more you consider the variables, the better the likely outcome. I wish I learned this earlier - but learn I did.

Vignette

I was assigned to work on a taskforce that was "studying the company for efficiencies." I was only a middle manager and being picked as a project leader was an indicator that I was being viewed "as Vice Presidential material." Healthy companies do these studies every few years to slaughter sacred cows that fattened unbeknownst to top management.

After a few months of this project, I presented the recommendations to senior management and was given the charge to implement the changes. I met with Joanne who was a VP in an operation that I had studied. Joanne was a savvy leader who was broadly respected. Joanne listened to my wisdom and indicated she understood everything I said and knew what had to be done. I left surprised that the meeting went so well.

A couple months later, I noticed that nothing had been done in Joanne's unit. I went back and asked Joanne why there had been no progress.

She said, "NIH."

"What is NIH?"

It means, "Not invented here."

I sat there still puzzled.

Joanne felt sorry for me and went on to explain that I had never involved her or her organization in my study. She explained that since the idea was "Not invented here," it couldn't be a good idea.

"But you said you understood and that they were good ideas."

"But I never said I would do them," she explained.

"Understanding and doing are two different things."

Nothing ever happened with my recommendations. I made a mistake by not involving the right people in the process. When I complained to senior management of this delay tactic, Joanne had already told them of her alternate plans that would save more money. She won the battle but I learned a lifetime lesson.

38. PETER PRINCIPLE

I ALWAYS THOUGHT THIS PHRASE was a polite way of saying someone was "a wiener." Since I didn't want to be viewed as the office sausage, I spent time studying all aspects of how/when/why managers maxed-out. There are many aspects of this principle to be considered. Ask yourself the following:

1. Am I really qualified for this higher position?
2. Am I setting myself up to fail?
3. If I fail, will I have other options afterwards?
4. If the job is a stretch, can I grow into it?
5. Will I enjoy the job?
6. I know I'll fail, but is the extra money and stature worth the pain?

These are questions that require mature and objective self-evaluation. I faced this dilemma a few times and said "no" to positions that would have been more prestigious. I also tried to avoid being offered positions that were negatives based on the above questions. Since senior leaders get puzzled and annoyed when "opportunities" are turned-down, you need to do so gracefully. Show the senior person great gratitude for considering you but leave no room for doubt. You can survive these career nightmares but there may be some initial coldness thereafter. It will pass.

Your career will fly by. During that trip, you will notice executives that "checked out" and are just there to collect a paycheck. Some of your peers aren't bothered by this situation, others are furious and some don't notice. I always noticed and didn't want to hang-on like a jock rash. All of us face a moment when we ask, "have I gone as far as I can?" All of us peak in a career and can manage the plateau with style. Think about it, stay alert and get out before someone tells you to.

Vignette

Al was a VP who was legendary for his ability to fire people. His nickname was "Dr. Death." He relished the tough reputation. Al had all sorts of tricks for canning people but his favorite was asking managers to meet him at an airport and giving them the bad news. Dr. Death often told his victims that they "were sick." When the manager protested that his/her health was fine, Al would clarify that, "You have to be sick or you wouldn't be doing such a lousy job."

One day I got a call from Al's administrator that he wanted to meet me at O'Hare airport. She went on to clarify that Al wanted to talk "about the job I was doing." It got worse. I had to be there right away because he didn't have a long layover. Needless to say, I needed to change my Jockeys before making the O'Hare trip. I tried to be positive but the dread set in.

As I approached Al, he greeted me with a huge grin. ("This is one sadistic son-of-a bitch", was what run through my mind.) I stood there ghostly pale as Al offered me a promotion working for him. As the words sunk-in, I stuttered an acceptance. As I gained my composure, I mentioned I thought he was there as "Dr. Death." Al got a tremendous laugh from my discomfort and told the story with glee for many years.

39. DOING WHAT'S RIGHT FOR THE COMPANY

GREAT LEADERS HAVE A REPUTATION for "doing what's right for the company." This sounds obvious but it isn't. What I mean is that you were willing to do something that hurts your own organization or career for the greater good of company results. You take the bullet so the platoon can take the hill. You are such a team player that selfless is too weak a word to describe your altruism.

The subtlety is making certain the right people know (and approve) of your decision. Never take for granted that the nobility was noticed. You have to tell senior leaders what you did and act like it was the only choice. Once you are certain the heroic move was noticed, don't dwell on it or mention it further. Act humbly and accept praise quietly. Walk the line carefully between tasteless self-promotion and classy team player.

Vignette

I was newly assigned to manage an east coast office. This was a stretch position for me because I didn't have any expertise in the product (Dental) that my office serviced. Corporate senior management was grooming me "for bigger jobs." All senior leaders were expected to have some operational background that "let them get their hands dirty."

My first week on the new job, I got a call that an important prospect wanted, " To meet with the people who would manage their business if they picked us." Since I knew nothing about Dental, I told the sales leader that I was a rookie and would be a liability. They told me, "Not to worry, they would handle any question I couldn't answer." Reluctantly, I agreed to go.

The customer visit was a nightmare. The questions were incredibly detailed and mostly pointed to me as "the man in charge of Dental service." The woman (Jane) representing the customer was relentless. Whenever someone tried to assist me, she said, "I'm not asking you! I want to hear what the Dental manager has to say. He's the one our employees will be depending on."

I'm not exaggerating. I literally knew no answers. This didn't daunt Jane. She kept drilling me. I furiously wrote down all the points I couldn't answer. When Jane stopped the interrogation, I said, "As you can probably tell, I'm new at my job and didn't prepare well enough. Bob (our sales leader) didn't want me on the team but I insisted. I apologize for my lack of background and assure you I will go get answers to all these points and return quickly. Don't judge our company by how poorly I did today."

Jane nodded politely but I could see she was unimpressed. When I returned with the information, Bob was talking about pricing. I knew the meeting had tanked when I noticed the consultant was sound asleep. His head was cocked back, arms hanging limply and mouth-breathing like he was trying to attract bugs into a Venus fly trap. When Bob was done, I mentioned that I had answers and proceeded to rattle them off. Jane listened but the consultant never stirred from his slumber. The meeting ended.

Bob was kind afterwards but agreed that it was the worst sales meeting in his career. That wasn't the fame I was looking for. I called my boss immediately and alerted him of the disaster. I took responsibility for the bomb but tried to mention my newness as a weak excuse. I didn't get much sympathy.

Early the next day, my boss called and said we had won

the business. He added that I was a big reason for the selection. Jane explained to our senior leader that, "His performance was almost pathetic, but he never quit. I liked his honesty and follow-up. Most people would have wilted under that pressure. He took accountability for his lack of knowledge. We knew your company didn't stock the sales team with phonies. We think you'll be good people to work with." Luck and honesty helped me dodge another bullet.

40. ORGANIZATIONAL CHANGE

I WAS ONCE ASKED what to do when your boss got canned in an organizational restructuring.

"Run like hell," was my reply. But if you can't…

If you reach an executive level, organizational changes happen every 2-3 years even in good times. If results are poor, it will happen quickly enough to give you whiplash. Since there is so much restructuring during a career, you must learn to manage it or it will manage you.

It surprised me how poorly my peers handled this mobile situation. Insecurity and ego often took the lead in their actions and doomed people rapidly. Many talented people just couldn't stand the uncertainty. They wanted definitive statements about their positions and those rarely came. Many bailed-out quickly and took mediocre jobs or left the reorganized company without another position secured. Friends of mine walked away from fortunes in stock options because they couldn't stand to wait.

Listed below are practices I followed religiously. At least one of these rules will work in any reorganization but some won't be needed every time. When you find yourself in this organizational dilemma, read this section carefully and decide what advice applies. All management changes have slightly different characteristics. Therefore the first rule is:

Go slowly

You will have a tendency to panic so take it easy. Determine if the change could cascade down to you. Were you overly loyal to the deposed boss? In an earlier section, Loyalty, I cautioned that this often led to blinding vision problems. If you think you were blindly loyal, you might have a problem. However, don't assume you will be let go quickly. HR people get involved and will slow the process down. It often takes months to evaluate people and this pause may give you time to maneuver. And then you must:

Work hard

Put your head down and make sure your results are strong. Then make certain that your new boss knows your work is going well. Management likes results and, if you deliver, you may survive. The non-performers are always the first to go. If they weren't loyal and they don't get the job done, why keep them? Then comes the next step.

Be visible

Once you get some credibility for good work, make certain you are visible. This is a good time to schedule time with the new boss and offer some ideas to improve the operation. Listen to how the leader reacts and volunteer to lead a project if he/she likes the suggestion. Be very engaged in meetings and be aggressive with your opinions. Watch your boss' body language and back off only if he/she seems to disagree. This isn't a time to be perceived as weak. If you get this far, you should do the following.

Create distance from the past

You have to be careful here, but try to create distance between you and deposed leadership. Make sure the new leader knows you disagreed with many previous strategies and had been vocal about this disagreement at that time. Let the boss know that you tried to prevent these past mistakes but were overruled. You hadn't walked blindly into the night.

Think like an alligator

This is the image and mindset you need to maintain. An alligator waits patiently, has thick skin, protects its territory and strikes when victory is likely. During organizational changes, you will eat a lot of crow (insert word of your choice) from the new leaders and diplomatic skills must rule your actions. Don't be mouthy or defensive.

Note that I worked for 26 bosses in 32 years and never got canned or demoted. Sometime I went sideways but I lived to fight again. You can survive organizational upheaval if you play the game well. Make a game of the challenge and take pride in small victories. Remember the next organizational change is only months away!

Vignette

Jim and I were peers and faced a nasty organizational change. Our boss (Mitch) was a close, personal friend with a top leader who protected Mitch for years. The top leader retired and Mitch got tired of the in fighting and left suddenly. Jim and I were clearly viewed as loyal to Mitch and new leadership was carefully reviewing us. Mitch was a curmudgeon and had many enemies. Most senior people wanted his whole regime "offed."

Jim and I got called in together to meet our new boss. We had no time to strategize or plan our story. I was sweating mentally if not physically. After a couple minutes, Jim made one of the craftiest moves I ever saw. He told the new boss, "Mitch was a coward and I'm glad he's gone. Once things got tough, he abandoned us. Everyone hated him and we're all glad he's gone."

The new manager just nodded his agreement as if there was nothing else to say. We chatted amiably and asked what we could do to help him succeed. We left the impression that we had just been liberated from an Iraqi prison. The boss relied on us immediately and we enjoyed a couple pleasant years. Jim went on to a great career and is planning his next survival line as we speak.

41. GOLF, WINE KNOWLEDGE, FINE DINING, ETC.

THESE HOBBIES ARE EXTREMELY VALUABLE assets to a career. While things like this may seem trivial and petty, don't underestimate their usefulness. When I started my sales career, I was told to learn golf. This advice wasn't a suggestion; it was an edict.

"Customers won't play tennis with you because you can kick their butt. Golf is for gentleman, tennis for jocks.

Golf is a tough game. I swallowed my pride and began the tortuous journey to learn the sport of gentleman. Like everyone else, I was horrible for a few years. I got lessons and made enough progress to break 100. Once you break this barrier, you can play with most people. Most customers were in my mediocre range and enjoyed having companionship while being humiliated by that damned little ball. I developed business relationships that my non-playing peers envied. "How come you can see that customer? They don't even return my call."

Because I played golf and they didn't. The customers like to get out of the office. Playing golf feels like getting a day off from school when you were a kid. It was sweet! Adults work hard and golf is an acceptable reason to play hooky. There is an implied assumption in the business world that you are somehow getting some cagey deal done on the links. Enough about golf; you got the idea.

I developed a keen interest in wine at an early age. I even write a monthly newsletter that is sent to friends, customers and others. It surprised me that customers were fascinated with wine. Once they learned I knew so much, they asked endless questions. Wine shops can be overwhelming and stuffy. I became the person they could ask questions that always bugged them. I had an edge.

Fine dining and wine are inseparable. We all love great meals. If you couple fabulous food with a unique wine, you have a memorable experience. How often have you been treated to a business dinner that you thought about for days? Not too often. If you learn to select great wines and find the better restaurants, you will never have your invitations declined. It's up to you. Get "Wine Spectator" and start reading.

Vignette

Dave was a challenging customer. He was smart, tough, demanding and liked being all of these traits. Our account reps couldn't get close to him and asked me to get involved. Dave was a golfer but wouldn't play during business hours. He didn't want anyone getting an edge on him.

Dave and I were going to an industry meeting and I called to see if he wanted to play golf on Sunday. Since we had to fly west (Arizona) on Sunday, for a Monday morning start time , why not get in a little earlier and shoot a round? Dave accepted but insisted on paying his way. "Will you pay for me too?" He liked the joke.

Dave was an athlete and a good golfer. He didn't get to play that often and was rusty. You could tell he would be very good if he played more. Work just got in the way. I was a decent player by then and we had a nice competition. We both liked ball busting and soon had an enjoyable time irritating each other.

As we approached one hole, I yelled to Dave that a bobcat was walking near the green. We watched this large cat stalking, then killing, a rabbit. My ball had landed near the killing zone, so I waited for the cat to disappear into the brush before approaching my ball. Just as I was about to hit, I heard a fierce howling behind me. I leaped in surprise!! (The only thing that kept me from skying higher was the load in my shorts.)

As I rushed to escape, I turned to find Dave laughing at my horror. He had mimicked the cat and was greatly delighting in my cowardice. It's tough to trick a trickster, but Dave nailed me. We still laugh about my high jump. It's hard to duplicate that camaraderie behind a desk.

42. BALANCE

"In business, you must choose between money and memories. I choose...?"

THIS BUSINESS AXIOM was recently quoted to me. The young executive was explaining that this was his choice and he was taking the money. "I'll catch up with the memories when my kids are older and we're wealthy."

No you won't!

The young man wasn't really looking for concurrence. He believed the two prizes were mutually exclusive. There was no way to balance a hectic work schedule and still maintain a normal family life. Sadly, too many executives follow this tragic thinking.

I believe you can have it all. I did it and you can too! It wasn't easy but I never missed my (3) children's activities. I never viewed my participation as an option. Here is how I approached this dilemma and gained control.

Family comes first

That was my starting maxim and everything flowed from there. The vast majority of business activity can be managed into a schedule. There will always be some perceived "critical" issue or meeting that arises and tries to prevent you from making your kid's ballgame, play, concert etc.

Make certain you are the one defining "critical"

Many workers spawn crisis because they procrastinated a task and a Herculean effort is needed to get back on track. I can hear you shaking your head in agreement. These knuckleheads live in a constant fire drill state. True crises are rare, must be accommodated, but can often be managed within your schedule.

Plan ahead

Build your family events into your schedule as early as possible. Ask for team schedules relentlessly. Be persistent and you can get coaches or school officials to show what's planned. It works.

Work odd hours

I came in earlier or worked later on days I went to family functions. Many times I left the school event and went back to work. All projects or assignments were completed Might be an hour early or later than preferred, but it got done. I never got a complaint from anyone important.

If you follow these precepts, you can have it all. There are people that live to work. I feel sorry for them and am convinced they will look back with regret. I never got a hug from flawlessly managed projects. Memories are forever.

Vignette

Lynn was a driven, talented peer. She was the bread-winner in the family and worked 24/7 before that phrase became popular. Lynn and I were rivals for a promotion and it became clear that she put in endless hours to get an edge. Not wanting to give in without a fight, I started coming in Saturday mornings to gain equal footing. Lynn was always there when I arrived and then mentioned that Sunday was even better "for catching up on industry reading." What to do?

After a few Saturdays of this nonsense, I stopped by

Lynn's office to say goodbye. As we were chatting, her phone rang and she picked it up. She got a concerned look on her face then got very agitated. It was obvious she was talking about one of her kids. It seemed to be a doctor on the other end. I got uncomfortable that the conversation was too personal and asked if she wanted me to leave.

"No, it's just Liz's psychiatrist. Can you believe it; he says she's anorexic and wants me to come in for a consultation? I'm trying to tell him that it's Bob's job." (Bob was her work-at-home husband.)

I just got up and left. Lynn looked puzzled as I walked out. That was my last Saturday in that horse race. I knew I couldn't keep pace with Lynn. Anyone who was irritated by a sick child was at some different plane from me. Lynn did get the promotion and works at the same pace today. She will probably get pissed off when asked to leave early for her own funeral.

SECTION 4

CONCLUSION

43. HARD WORK

I SAVED THE MOST OBVIOUS FOR LAST. Without hard work, competitiveness and confidence, you spin as aimlessly as Tommy Lee and Madonna at a Mensa meeting.

Hard work is a vital ingredient of success. To be successful, you have to outwork your competition. If you foolishly insist on a steady, dependable pace, clouds of dust will smack your face as your hustling peers pass you by. When anything important hits your desk, you need to go into turbo drive.

Hard work is woven into all of the other skills mentioned in this book, and it is the backbone of them all. People often trick themselves that they are working hard. There can't be any doubt or trickery. You have to bust your butt.

I used to describe my workday as a long run. There were some sprints and some steady trots. I never walked or stood still. At the end of my day, I was breathing deeply and had beads of sweat on my brow. Look yourself in the mirror and make sure you are making the effort to be a winner.

44. COMPETITIVENESS

I AM VERY COMPETITIVE by nature. I viewed every assignment as an opportunity to do better than my peers. I wanted my team to win whether the task was a charity drive, Halloween decorating contest, having the best office location or achieving some critical part of the business plan. People like to win and your team will get an extra boost of pride when they come out on top.

There can also be an unhealthy level of competition. I never sabotaged a peer or played dirty. I used competition as a way to focus my team and to have some fun. Work gets tedious sometimes and a splash of competition can get your people juiced. There are just too few moments when you hear and feel adrenaline rushing through your staff. Used effectively, competition can give your unit an edge.

45. CONFIDENCE

PEOPLE ARE DRAWN to confident leaders. Even when they are worried or uncertain, the confident leaders never show doubt. Even when things go wrong, this sturdy leader brushes failure aside and prepares for upcoming success. This charismatic leader gives you the feeling that only minor adjustments and hard work is needed to succeed.

Don't ignore or underestimate the power of confidence. If you act hesitantly, your team will sense your doubt and will falter. If you act with purpose and certainty, the team will forge ahead relentlessly. Even ill conceived tasks can be miraculously done if a motivated team acts with common purpose and resolve. The bus may be headed in the wrong direction, but it is moving fast and get can you home.

Great leaders have different sources of this confident strength. It may be brilliant planning, unshakable senior support or tremendous knowledge of the business. Whatever the wellspring, these gifted leaders think they are right. Something may go wrong, but they are undeterred. Ultimately, they plan to win and are certain they will win. People like a sure thing.

46. LUCK

MANY PEOPLE WALK AROUND believing that luck separates the winners and losers. I frequently heard "you're the kind of guy that steps in shit and comes out smelling like a rose." The unspoken message was that luck was responsible for my success and I just sat there and reaped the harvest.

Bullshit!

I get annoyed when people think they are victims of fate and can do nothing about it. There are unfortunate events in everyone's life and how you react to "bad luck" defines much of your character. It is easier to be bitter and defeatist rather than picking yourself up and fighting back. Here is my view and approach on luck:

1) People that work hard seem to be luckier than most.

2) Defining moments happen rarely in a career. Are you able to spot these unique moments of opportunity? Lucky people

have good vision.

3) Do you capitalize on these defining moments and catapult your career? I knew when they occurred for me and made certain I took full advantage.

4) Can you turn misfortune into career momentum? Do you wallow in failure or show the boss and peers that you rebound like Wilt Chamberlain?

5) Surround yourself with "lucky people." My friends are all positive, upbeat and successful. They love life and don't wait for things to happen. Luck is contagious.

6) If an approach doesn't work, change direction. The term "beating things to death" was invented for good reason. Lots of people never swerve from a losing course.

Vignette:

My wife and I were enjoying a peaceful golf outing on a lazy Saturday afternoon. It was one of those days where you just loved being there and didn't care much about how you played. Now that I painted this benign picture, here is how it went to hell.

I hit an errant shot into the woods. To get back in the fairway, I needed a miracle shot through the trees. I decided to go for it and launched a ferocious shot. The good news is it made it through the trees. The bad news is it veered to the right and headed into the wrong fairway at a woman in a floppy sun hat. I yelled "fore" and watched the lady drop to her knees as the ball knocked her hat for a perfect triple flip.

I hurried up to make amends and saw the President of my company standing over his fallen wife. She was unhurt except for being stunned. My life (and career) passed before my eyes. I apologized profusely, and they were very polite, but I could tell they were unhappy. I didn't know the President very well and had visions of being remembered as "the asshole that decked my wife." This was clearly an "unlucky situation." What to do?

I went to a Hallmark store and looked for funny golf cards. I found a gem of a stunned golfer, lying on the ground, with a golf ball solidly planted in the bull's eye in the middle of his forehead. The card caption said, "I didn't think this was what 'target golf' meant." I addressed the card to the President's wife, apologized sincerely, and ended with "this isn't the type of impression I wanted to leave."

The President and his wife loved the card and we became friends and golf buddies. We still laugh about the unfortunate incident. Was this good luck or bad luck for me? It could have been an immense dose of bad luck, if I let it sit. However, I thought it through, and then took a chance that these people had a sense of humor and were gracious by nature. I didn't accept being memorialized as "an asshole." I don't think luck had anything to do with the outcome.

And:

This is the miraculous way I became successful. Much of my approach was common sense and hard work. There is a surprising lack of common sense in business. It really should be called "uncommon sense."

I didn't settle with things as they were. They could always be better. I tried to adjust and adapt to what came at me. I looked at failure as more a lack of effort than some innate weakness. Push hard enough and things tend to fall in place.

Be confident but don't be cocky. Act pleasantly surprised when things go as planned. Expect your career to be good but don't get down or bitter when something goes awry. When you get in a bad work stretch, remember that the good stuff is just some hard work away.

Keep your eyes open and grab that next opportunity!